Map of Wimbledon, *c.*1740 by John Roque.

WIMBLEDON
A Pictorial History

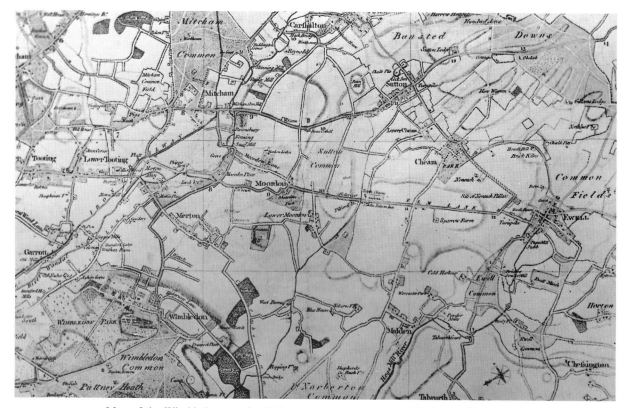

Map of the Wimbledon area in 1819. An unusual projection with the south at the top.

WIMBLEDON
A Pictorial History

Richard Milward

With best wishes,
Richard Milward

Phillimore

1994

Published by
PHILLIMORE & CO. LTD.
Shopwyke Manor Barn, Chichester, Sussex

ISBN 0 85033 945 6

Printed and bound in Great Britain by
BIDDLES LTD.
Guildford, Surrey

List of Illustrations

Frontispiece: Map of Wimbledon Area, 1819

Acknowledgements

To the Wimbledon Society Museum Committee for permission to make full use of their fine collection of old photographs, from which the vast majority of the pictures in this book have been taken. I am especially grateful for the help of Lady Hartopp (President of the Society), Norman Plastow (its Chairman), Bernard Rondeau (Curator of Photographs), Alan Elliot (Curator of Ephemera), Paul Bowness, Connie Curry and David Heaton. Without their invaluable support this book could not have been produced.

To all those who have kindly given me permission to use their photographs: Judy Goodman of the John Innes Society, 77; Hunting Aerofilms, 3, 43; Mr. Jefferys, 109, 110; Merton Library Service, 56, 59; Bob North, 99; James Russell & Sons, St Mark's Place, 103, 131; Barry Turner, 173, 177.

And to Sue Coley who has typed the manuscript with her usual efficiency.

Part I Historical Outline

Introduction: The London Borough of Merton

Officially Wimbledon no longer exists. For four centuries its inhabitants had governed themselves, but at midnight on 31 March 1965 their town was merged with Merton, Mitcham and Morden to form a new London Borough of Merton. The change was far from popular. It was described as 'a shot-gun marriage' and there was genuine dismay at the dropping of the internationally-known 'Wimbledon' for the relatively unknown name of 'Merton'.

Over the intervening years the new Merton Council has made a number of controversial changes in the town. Perhaps the most far-reaching came in 1985: the removal of its headquarters from Wimbledon to Crown House, Morden. The Town Hall was sold and transformed into a shopping mall christened Centre Court. The Civic Hall next door was pulled down and not replaced. The fire station and Magistrates Courts were moved elsewhere. The town was thus deprived of its old centre.

Yet Wimbledon has managed to preserve its separate identity. The Common has given the area a special attraction. The Tennis Championships have made the place known all over the world. Above all, its history has provided Wimbledon with its own individual character. The men and women who have lived here over the centuries, the buildings they have put up and the society they have created have all slowly fashioned a community whose loyalties even modern planners have proved unable to change.

1 Wimbledon's second Town Hall, 1988. Designed by A.J. Hope, it cost about £200,000 and was opened by Prince George, later Duke of Kent, in 1931. It was criticised by the architectural historian, Professor Pevsner, as 'stone-faced, symmetrical and dull', but at least it looked more like a genuine civic centre than its successor, Crown House, Morden. In May 1988 it was the focus for the large crowds which welcomed the return from Wembley of the Wimbledon Football team with the F.A. Cup.

Early Wimbledon

From earliest times men and women have settled in the Wimbledon area. The large high plateau in the north-western half of the parish on which lies the Common was hardly fertile, yet it was well-drained and had a good water supply. The land below the crown of the hill, though heavy clay, proved suitable for growing wheat or pasturing cattle. The parish, however, did not lie on any natural line of communication. So for centuries the few settlers remained remote and isolated.

The discovery of Neolithic arrowheads and knives on the Common and of Bronze Age round-barrows near the Portsmouth Road may show only that the plateau was then used for hunting and for burying the dead. But the building on its south-western edge of a large hill-fort with a deep ditch and 20-foot high rampart probably in the early Iron Age is a sure sign that the plateau's natural defensive advantages were also appreciated. This so-called 'Caesar's Camp' was not used for long, however, and was certainly never occupied by Julius Caesar.

For the next thousand years Wimbledon has no recorded history. The Romans came to Putney and Merton. Early Saxon warriors settled in Mitcham. Neither seem to have shown any interest in the land in between, though a few Roman coins, a sling stone and the fragment of a vase have been found in the area.

2   A painting by F.C. Nightingale of Caesar's Camp, 1 July 1865. The early Iron Age ditch and ramparts are still very evident, even with their covering of trees. Only ten years later the trees were cut down and the ramparts levelled on the orders of the owner, John Erle-Drax, M.P., after he had been prevented from building houses on the site.

3 An aerial view of the Camp, *c*.1923. The near circular outline of the defences is just visible to the left of the houses Drax did build in 1870. Across the Camp runs a public right of way through the Royal Wimbledon Golf Course. To the north west, in the middle of a dark circle of trees, is Caesar's Well. In the bottom left-hand corner is Warren Farm.

The Medieval Manor

At some time in the seventh or eighth century Wimbledon became part of a manor owned by the Archbishop of Canterbury. Its original name, 'Wimbedounyng' or 'Wunemannedun' mentioned in charters, suggests that it may originally have been established by a Saxon called Wynnman. But it is impossible to say where the village was situated or even whether there was a group of cottages sufficiently large to be described as a village. All that can be said for certain is that in 1086, when the Domesday Survey was made, there was 'a church' there, probably on the site of the present St Mary's, the mother church of the Archbishop's manor of Mortlake, which included Putney and Barnes as well as Wimbledon.

By the 13th century the Archbishop had a large farm near the church, producing corn, hay, fruit, wool, cheese and even wine. His bailiffs employed six ploughmen, a cowherd, a shepherd and two carters. His tenants, who tilled plots in the large open field below the Ridgway and grazed their animals on the Common, had to work for him for part of the year, particularly during the harvest. The lives of these 'villeins' were dominated by a Manor Court which regulated their use of the fields and the Common, as well as enforcing law and order, repair of the roads and the punishment of drunkards, 'common gossips and disturbers of the peace'.

How many people lived in the medieval parish is uncertain. Before the Black Death of 1348 there may have been as many as two hundred. The dreaded plague, however, was so lethal that as late as 1437 only half the arable land could be cultivated and a large area to the south of Copse Hill had become 'overgrown with bramble, thorn and furze'. Indeed it is likely that the population did not exceed two hundred again until the reign of Henry VIII.

The plague, however, benefited the survivors. They no longer had to work for the Archbishop; instead they paid rent for their plots of land. Some became yeomen farmers with 15 to 30 acres. Others, notably the Lewston family, owned estates of over two hundred acres. By 1500 Wimbledon was again so prosperous that the Archbishop, Cardinal Morton, had the first brick house built near the church. Now known as the Old Rectory, it may have been intended as a palace for the Archbishop. Instead it was used by the Rectors of St Mary's until the Reformation.

4 'An old farm near St Mary's', drawn by William Porden in 1810, just before it was pulled down. It was probably situated where Burghley and Church Roads meet today. In the Middle Ages it had been the 'curia' or headquarters of the Archbishops' bailiffs. Later it became the home of the farmer who looked after the Lord of the Manor's park and fields.

5 The Old Rectory, *c*.1970. It is the oldest house in Wimbledon, the first to be built in brick and originally much larger. The only surviving parts of the early Tudor building are the hall and bedrooms, as well as parts of the two spiral staircases. Beyond the hedge on the right of the picture lies St Mary's churchyard.

The Four Manor Houses

Henry VIII's break with the Pope started the transformation of Wimbledon from an obscure backwater into a place described in 1826 as 'a highly respectable village, the preferred residence of many of our representatives and nobility'.

The first noble family to settle here were the Cecils. In 1536 Archbishop Cranmer surrendered the manor to Henry, together with the Rectory and control of the parish church. During the reigns of Edward VI and Mary the Rectory was leased to a rising politician, Sir William Cecil, as a country retreat. His eldest son, Thomas, was brought up there and so liked the place that he too settled in the house with his family. In 1588, the year of the Armada, he built a magnificent new manor house on the slope of the hill to the east of the Rectory. Only fifty years later the Cecil family sold the manor house and park to Charles I's wife, Queen Henrietta Maria. At the end of the Civil War the estate was seized by Parliament and sold to one of Cromwell's leading generals, John Lambert. In 1677 it became a country retreat of Charles II's chief minister, Thomas Osborne Earl of Danby, but by the time he died, 35 years later, the Elizabethan manor house had fallen into disrepair.

Its new owner, a wealthy Huguenot financier, Sir Theodore Janssen, decided in 1717 to demolish it and use the bricks to build a second more modest manor house in the latest Georgian style. He chose a different site, west of St Mary's church, but the house was barely completed when he was involved in a big financial scandal and lost most of his fortune including the Wimbledon estates.

Sarah Churchill, Duchess of Marlborough, was responsible for the third manor house. In 1724 she bought the Wimbledon Park estate together with the lordship of the manor and decided to build a large Palladian mansion in grey brick on top of the plateau above the site of the Elizabethan house. When she died in 1744 she left it to her favourite grandson, John Spencer. His son, the first Earl Spencer, employed 'Capability' Brown to create 'one of the finest parks in England' with a large ornamental lake, coverts for shooting and a new carriage way from the Portsmouth Road. This house, however, was destroyed by fire in 1785.

The second Earl Spencer waited 14 years before commissioning Henry Holland to build the fourth manor house, a large villa near the site of Sarah's mansion. It had some fine rooms, a wonderful view to the south from the portico and a very deep well which soon silted up. In 1828, however, the Spencer family left the house for good and 18 years later sold it along with the park to John Augustus Beaumont, a property developer.

The interest shown in Wimbledon by three of the greatest families in England, the Cecils, the Churchills and the Spencers, played a crucial part in the growth of the village. Their great mansions needed an army of servants, as well as constant repairs and improvements, often carried out by local craftsmen. Their custom was also valuable for village shopkeepers who were asked to supply the great house with food. Above all, their contacts with the Court, the Government and the City led important officials or rich merchants to follow their example and use Wimbledon as a country retreat. One of the earliest was Robert Bell, a founder of the East India Company, who in 1613 built a fine mansion in the High Street, now known as Eagle House.

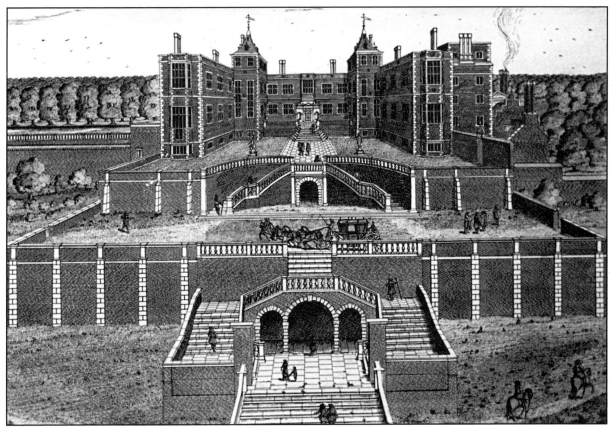

6 The front view of the Cecil manor house drawn by Henry Winstanley in 1678. It had an equally impressive interior. To the left of the main door was 'a fair and large hall' with state rooms and a chapel in the wing beyond. Up the stairs in the tower was a long gallery with a fine view over the park. At the top of the tower was a large cistern which provided the house with water.

7 View from the garden, also by Winstanley. To the right of the house the entrance drive goes straight across the park towards the road to London. In the foreground the garden rises in a series of terraces to a plateau where the later houses were built.

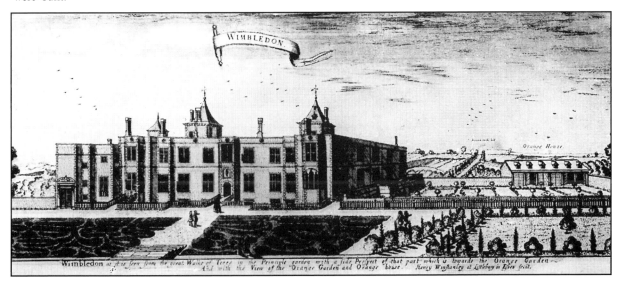

8 The second manor house, 1900, just before it was pulled down. It was designed by Colen Campbell with only two storeys, but a third was added later. In 1834 James Courthope Peache renamed it Belvedere House after the road in Lambeth where he ran his timber business. In the centre of this picture of the garden front are the large stables, parish church and entrance lodge.

9 The Marlborough manor house, from *Vitruvius Brittanicus*. Designed for the gouty Duchess of Marlborough by Lord Henry Herbert and Roger Morris, the ground floor was sunk into a hollow so that she could go into the front door on the floor above without having to go up steps. Inside were beautifully furnished rooms with fine views over the country both to north and south.

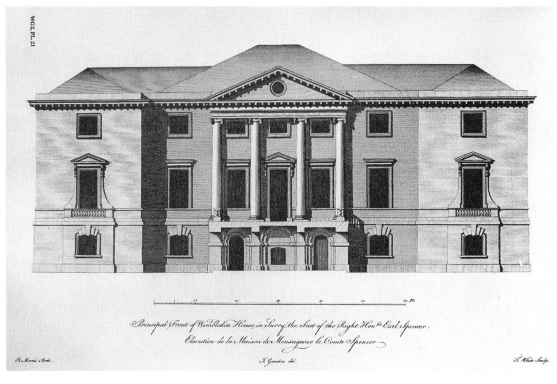

10 The Spencer manor house, drawn by William Porden, c.1815. Its portico looks out over the lawns with a ha-ha in the foreground. Behind the bow-window to the left was the drawing room and above were the main bedrooms. To the rear were the kitchens and servants' quarters. It was pulled down in 1948. Twenty-four years later Park House Middle School was built on the site.

11 The domed Well House, Arthur Road, 1912. It covers a well originally dug to a depth of 30 to 40 feet. In 1796 Earl Spencer had it dug much deeper. At a depth of 563 feet the workmen struck water which shot up over 100 feet and nearly drowned them. But the well was not properly constructed. It slowly silted up and had to be abandoned soon after 1815. Recently it has been transformed into a delightful residence.

12 Gap Lodge, 1885. An unusual photograph of one of the entrance lodges to the Spencer manor house. It was built in the 1860s to cover a gap in the park pale where intruders had regularly climbed in to poach the game. The path in the foreground later became Leopold Road, developed in the 1890s and named after one of Queen Victoria's sons.

The Georgian Village

The influence of the Spencer family on the growth of the village in the reign of George III is well illustrated by an unusual map. Drawn in 1776 for the first Earl and entitled 'Sketch of the Town of Wimbledon', it is similar to a modern Underground map, without scale and fitting in as much as possible on a series of fairly straight roads. It records almost every house and lists their occupants and jobs (suggesting that about 1,000 people were then living in Wimbledon, double the number in 1744).

Signs of growing prosperity can be seen in the plan of the High Street. It shows posts at the side of the road to protect both pedestrians and houses from the increase in traffic, including the 'Wimbledon Machine', a short-stage coach which travelled up to London three days a week. It also lists more shops than thirty years earlier, some in buildings so substantial that they survive on the western side of the road today. A further sign of prosperity can be found in local documents which show that Wimbledon was drawing many 'strangers' looking for work.

A great deal of the work was provided by 'gentlemen' (many of them friends of the Spencer family) who were settling in new houses which the map marks round the Common. Among them were leading members of Parliament, including one Prime Minister (the Marquis of Rockingham who died here in 1782) and two Cabinet Ministers (William Grenville at Eagle House, 1787-8, and Henry Dundas at Cannizaro, 1785-1806). Together with William Wilberforce (who owned Lauriston House, 1777-86), Grenville and Dundas frequently entertained the young Prime Minister, William Pitt, who came to regard Wimbledon as his second home. In addition, one of Pitt's chief opponents, John Horne Tooke, was living at Chester House (1792-1812), while important French exiles, Charles de Calonne (1789-91) and the Prince of Condé (1810-15) leased Wimbledon House Parkside.

None of these great men played any real part in local affairs. Their main interests lay in London and normally they stayed in Wimbledon only during the summer. But they brought much wealth and prestige to the area and made it an important centre of Georgian society. King George III often held military reviews on the Common, especially during the Wars with Revolutionary France, and went on to have a late breakfast with Dundas at Cannizaro.

By the time of the first census in 1801 the population had risen to nearly 1,600. Many were poor and 'in the greatest distress', owing to a sharp rise in the cost of food during the wars and to 'want of employment' afterwards. In addition, smallpox was reported to be 'very prevalent' in 1817. Attempts were made to help poor families by providing bread, potatoes and 'coals' at a reduced price and by building small cottages along the Ridgway at low rents. But the only lasting success was against smallpox. John Sanford, an apothecary who lived at Ashford House, insisted on inoculating many of the poor and so made the village a healthier place in which to live.

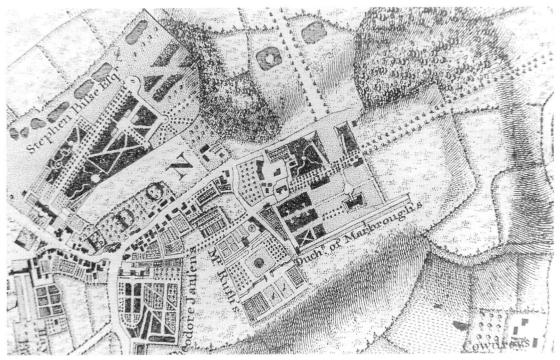

13 Map of Wimbledon in the 1740s by John Rocque. The village lies to the left along the High Street. The large building to the north with the ornamental park and fish ponds is Wimbledon House Parkside; the two smaller buildings just below it are the *Rose and Crown* inn and Eagle House. The new Marlborough manor house is shown in its 'saucer'. St Mary's church is right in the centre with the graveyard wall round it.

14 The High Street, *c*.1875. The earliest known photograph of the area, with the *Rose and Crown* to the left and the new buildings of the *Dog and Fox* in the background. In the middle of the road is one of the original London omnibuses with a door and step at the back. Most of the shops on the right were built in the late 18th century and are still there.

15 The front of Wimbledon House Parkside in 1815, just after it had been bought by Joseph Marryat M.P., father of the novelist, Captain Frederick Marryat. The grounds were developed by Mrs. Marryat into one of the finest gardens near London.

16 Herbert Mason (1828-1917) tending plants in the front garden of Holly Cottage, 6 The Green, c.1910. His family had been leading tradesmen in the village since the 1750s. His father, William (1808-91), was a baker in the High Street, who celebrated his golden wedding with his six children and 13 grandchildren present. Like his father, Herbert described himself as 'a gentleman'.

17 The Crooked Billet, *c.*1900. Originally a small collection of cottages to the west of the Common, it takes its name from the pub whose sign is in the centre of the photo. The buildings behind the washing are the Cinque Cottages, built in 1872 by Sir Henry Peek M.P. to house 'poor men of good character in needy circumstances and not less than fifty-five'.

18 Chester House, Westside: the garden front, *c.*1920. The house dates back to the reign of William and Mary, and like many great houses had a fine garden. In 1993 this was destroyed to make way for Lordell Place, named after the first owner. The origin of the name of Chester House is unknown.

19 Cannizaro House, Westside: the garden front under alteration, 1920s. The house, built in Queen Anne's reign, was seriously damaged by fire in 1900. The front facing the Common and the interior had to be completely reconstructed, but the fine garden front with its bay window was saved. In the 1920s the two main downstairs rooms were enlarged, hence the gaping holes in the wall.

20 Warren Farm, *c*.1910. The buildings on the western edge of the Common overlooking Beverley Brook were originally the home of a warrener who looked after the highly-prized rabbits and deer in the Elizabethan Old Park. They were later made into a farm whose land covered the modern Royal Wimbledon Golf course. They are now a very pleasant private house and are more difficult to see than in 1910.

21 Woodhayes House and garden, 1902. The house, built *c*.1760, bears a striking resemblance to the octagonal school put up in Camp Road at the same time. Its garden originally extended to the Ridgway, but in 1904 most of the estate was sold for building. The house was pulled down *c*.1970 and town houses laid out round Peregrine Way.

22 An old lodge to Cottenham Park House, *c.*1905, at the bottom of Durham Road. It had probably been built *c.*1830 when the Earl of Cottenham took over the mansion, till then known as Prospect Place. By 1905 it was the home of 'W. Anderson. Sanitary Plumber'. It was pulled down *c.*1930 and a block of shops built on the site. One is now a launderette.

23 Prospect Place, *c.*1780, facing east with a coach arriving from the direction of the later Durham Road. By 1800 it was the centre of a large estate extending from Copse Hill to Coombe Lane. In 1852 it was sold for development. Its site is now covered by the laundry and bus stop for Atkinson Morley's Hospital.

A Railway Suburb

On 21 May 1838 Wimbledon's relative isolation was broken for ever. A primitive railway engine pulling a few coaches passed through the tiny station isolated in the fields at the bottom of the hill. It came from Nine Elms near Vauxhall and went on to Woking via Surbiton. At first the trains had little effect on life in the village but, as additional lines were opened to West Croydon, Epsom, Tooting and Kingston between 1855 and 1869, Wimbledon became an important railway junction.

Already in 1850 a piped water supply had been laid in the valley by the Lambeth Water Company from its reservoir at Thames Ditton. At the same time land in South Wimbledon was relatively cheap and building societies, especially the British Land Company, were ready to finance its development, as there was a big demand for new houses south of London. Professional men who worked in the City were attracted to Wimbledon by its good train service and its healthy open spaces. Working-class families were also attracted there from Inner London or the Home Counties by the prospect of work—on the railway, on building sites, in shops, as gardeners or in domestic service.

As a result, in just fifty years Wimbledon was transformed from a growing village into a major suburb of London. In 1861 the population had been about 4,600. By 1911 it had increased well over tenfold to 55,000. South of the railway 'New Wimbledon' had been created with streets like Gladstone and Russell Roads lined by small terraced houses. The manual workers living there had to support their families on only about a pound a week. Many suffered from periods of unemployment; their children were affected by epidemics of scarlet fever, typhoid and diphtheria. North of the railway professional families often lived in large Victorian houses lining new roads off Worple, the Ridgway or Parkside. Many owned a horse-drawn carriage and employed a number of servants (there were over 5,000 of them in Wimbledon by 1911, a tenth of the population). They also enjoyed many sources of entertainment, including musical evenings and cycling, which became a craze in the 1890s.

At about this time West Wimbledon at last began to be developed. It was opened up, not by the building of Raynes Park station in 1871, but by the extension of Worple Road to Raynes Park 20 years later and the start of a tram service from Kingston and Hampton Court in 1907. Parts of Cottenham Park and the Drax estate, however, were still countrified long after the end of the First World War.

By then Wimbledon was no longer a fast-growing suburb. Its population remained stable at around 57,000, while the areas 'ripe for development' were now to the south: at Cannon Hill, Morden and Motspur Park. Instead it became, in the words of the official guide book, 'the ideal residential area' for young families, with 'unrivalled rail and road services', good schools and 'our proudest heritage, the Common'.

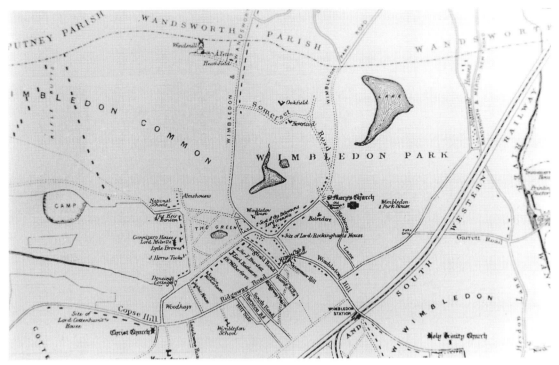

24 A map of Wimbledon, 1865. It shows the start of the railway suburb, with the first houses and roads of 'New Wimbledon', the first roads south of the Ridgway, the first Victorian houses along Copse Hill and above all the development of Wimbledon Park with large mansions along Parkside and Somerset Road. It also marks the 'Rifle Butts' for N.R.A. meetings on the Common.

25 The railway bridge, *c*.1925, with the top of Hartfield Road to the left. The original platform of 1838 is well to the left of the bridge. The new station on the London side was built in the 1880s, with a District Line station just to the north added in 1889. The original iron bridge over the railway remained until shops were added in the early 1930s.

26 Newstead, Somerset Road, *c.*1925. Built in the 1850s when Beaumont began to develop Wimbledon Park, it was bought by John Murray, a publisher, and named after the home of Lord Byron whose poems his father had published. Famous Victorians like Mr. Gladstone and Jenny Lind were entertained here. The site is now covered by the town houses of Newstead Way.

27 The Village Green in 1906. Once a triangular piece of open land, in the late 18th century houses like Holly Cottage were put up on the southern half, opposite the end of the High Street. The rest of the Green remained open until 1906. Then it too was developed, despite the protests of the newly-founded John Evelyn Club.

High Street, Wimbledon.

28 The southern part of the High Street, *c*.1905, before the shops on the east had been built. The land here had been part of the Belvedere estate which was sold for development in 1900. The fine London and County (now Westminster) Bank building was then put up at the corner of the new Belvedere Grove. The drinking fountain in the foreground had been erected in 1868 as a memorial to Joseph Toynbee, a distinguished ear and throat specialist and a founder of the Village Club.

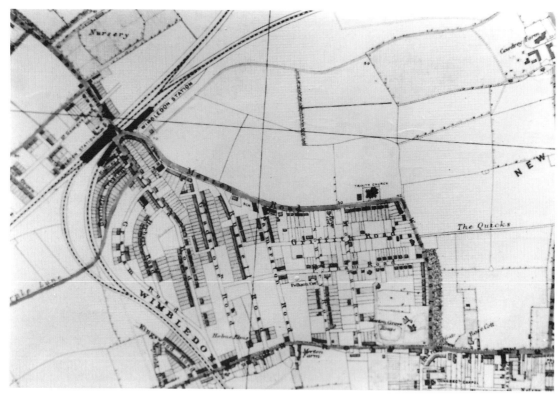

29 A map of New Wimbledon, 1877, showing the rapid development of the land to the south of Merton Road (now the Broadway). To the north are the fields of Cowdray Farm, crossed by The Quicks, a right of way marking the northern boundary of Nelson's Merton Place estate. Worple Road has its first houses, while Thomson's Nursery covers the site of the present library and post office.

30 Cows grazing in a field between the future Gladstone and Palmerston Roads in the 1860s. The right of way behind them was soon to become Palmerston Road. In the background are the first houses in Griffith and Pelham Roads.

31 The Broadway from the air, *c*.1920, with little traffic on the roads. The dome of the Theatre is at the bottom of the picture. The spires of the Congregational and Presbyterian churches rise north of the railway, while the front of the Baptist church dominates the first Town Hall to the south of the station.

32 The Broadway at Christmas time, 1908. A puzzling picture: what exactly is the cart from Tooting advertising: 'Santa Claus and Teddy Bears State Visit to the children'? The shops are decorated with flags, while in the background the Town Hall has a large banner on the balcony which seems to read 'Welcome'—to whom?

Christmastime at Wimbledon.

33 Children paddling in the river by Wandle Park during the summer of 1912. The Park had been opened five years earlier by Princess Louise, Duchess of Argyll. In the years before the First World War it was very popular as a 'holiday resort', but later fell into decay.

34 The bottom of Hill Road, c.1900, before the trams arrived. The shops on the right include Genoni's restaurant and George Ely 'provision merchant'. Up the hill are trees in front of the Library. On the left is one of Wimbledon's earliest estate agents, Ogdens. Further on are Edwin Trim's offices and printing works (where the Midland Bank is today) and Joseph Ely's second shop on the corner of Worple Road.

35 Tram lines being laid in St George's Road, c.1905. On the right is the entrance to the Drill Hall and beyond the offices of the *Wimbledon Borough News*. On the left are a number of small shops and up the steps the entrance to Spencer College, where the back entrance to Elys is today. The original 'Elys, Outfitter's' shop lies behind the awning at the corner of Alexandra Road.

36 Hill Road, *c*.1922. On the right are Bank Buildings, put up in the middle 1880s. Opposite are the many small shops with distinctive first-floor windows, built at about the same time. A horse-drawn coal cart is coming down the road in front of a tram, just starting for the Embankment from its terminus at the bottom of the hill. (The terminus was changed to the Town Hall in 1932.)

37 The remains of Thomson's Nursery, *c*.1910. On the right at the corner of Alwyne Road is the home of Robert Thomson, architect son of the nurseryman. Beyond is the 'spacious conservatory' of David Thomson who came to Wimbledon in 1838 and designed many large gardens in the area. Up the hill on the right Jack, the trace horse, can just be seen waiting to help another cart.

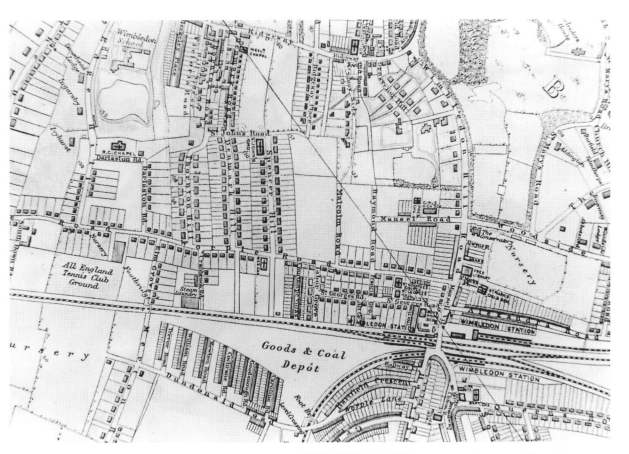

38 A map of Worple Road area, 1890. Since 1877 a line of middle-class houses has gone up along almost the entire length of the road (which until 1891 ended at the bottom of Arterberry Road). David Thomson has also moved his main nursery south of the railway to the west of Merton Hall Road, where it remained until compulsorily purchased in 1920 for house building.

39 A watercolour by Emily Bardswell of Worple Road in 1874, painted at the bottom of Thornton Hill. A shepherd drives a small flock of sheep along what was then a narrow country lane. Hidden to the left lies a field recently leased by the All-England Croquet Club, which in 1877 staged its first tennis championship.

40 The corner of Hill and Worple Roads in 1906, just before trams arrived. To enable them to turn, the first shops on the north of Worple Road were literally cut in half. To protect their open fronts, hoardings were put up and were soon covered with posters advertising the first 'animated pictures' at the Worple Hall, in the background of the picture.

41 The eastern end of Worple Road, *c.*1910, with trams now in operation. On the right are Elys and some small shops, including a barber where Sainsbury's is today. On the left are the truncated shops with their fronts restored and the Wimbledon Arcade with its shops, Worple Hall and skating rink. In the background is the *Queen Alexandra* pub.

42 Workmen in Worple Road (between Edge Hill and Darlaston Road) *c*.1905. They are putting the iron poles in place to support tram wires. They have already widened the road by taking a large slice out of the gardens on the south side.

43 An aerial view of Worple Road during the All-England Championships of 1920. The centre court and grounds are far from full, yet Edge Hill, Darlaston Road and Midmoor Road are lined by parked cars. To the south of the railway, Thomson's Nursery has been dismantled.

44 The Ridgway to the west of Edge Hill, *c*.1905. On the left is the so-called 'Lovers' Gate', the entrance to Wright's Alley, with the fence and hedge of King's College playing field beyond. On the right is the fence in front of Ridgelands owned by Colonel Longstaff, a patron of Antarctic explorers, especially Captain Scott.

45 Map of Wimbledon Park in 1882, showing Arthur, Home Park, Leopold, Strathearn and Wimbledon Park Roads already laid out, but with few properties yet sold. Ashen Grove Farm is marked just to the left of 4. The *Woodman Tavern* is to the right of 3.

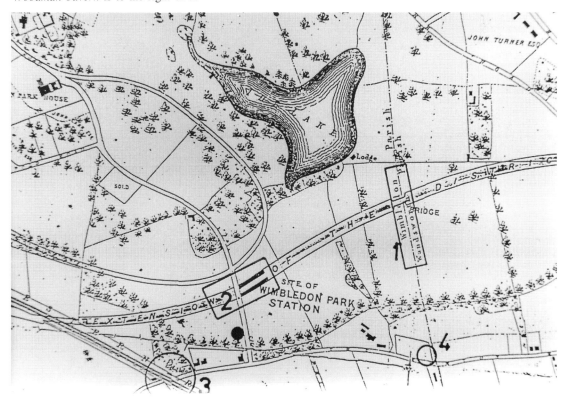

46 Wimbledon Park Lake and Golf Course, *c.*1920, saved from development in 1914 when they were bought by the Council. Home Park Road in the foreground has yet to be made up. Many of the trees are still there, but the old boat house by the lake has gone, as has the original Club House on the right, destroyed by a V-1 flying bomb in 1944.

47 The shops in Arthur Road, *c.*1917. They had been built 11 years earlier, including the post office, run by Alderman Shirl Mussell, later Mayor of Wimbledon. The District Line station of 1889 lies behind the errand-boy's bicycle on the left.

48 St Luke's Church of England parish church being built in 1908. Behind the large notice board new houses are also going up in Ryfold Road. In the background is the long corrugated building used by Wimbledon Park Elementary School.

49 Marlborough (now Stroud) Road, *c.*1915. The houses were built in 1906-7 with iron railings and gates which had to be sacrificed in 1940 to help the war effort. The Wimbledon Park Farm milk cart has a large churn with different measures hung round the side.

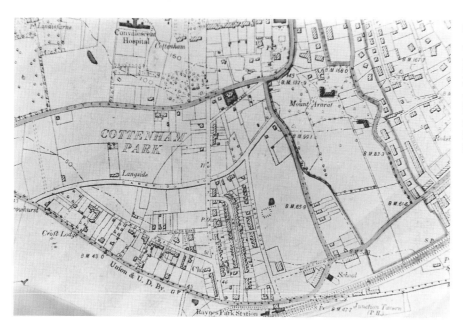

50 Map of Cottenham Park in 1893. It covers two large estates: The Earl of Cottenham's between Copse Hill and Coombe Lane (broken up in 1852) and Thomas Devas's based on Mount Ararat (only broken up in 1900). The development of this land was greatly helped by the extension of Worple Road through the Devas estate in 1891.

51 An aerial view of West Wimbledon in 1919, taken by Captain L. Hutcheon, R.A.F., who lived in Pepys Road. On the right is the Ridgway with K.C.S. playing fields and beyond the Drax estate. In the centre are the roads linking the Ridgway to Worple Road on the far left, some like Ridgway Place with a lot of empty plots. In the middle stands Wimbledon College and the Sacred Heart church. In the background are the fields of the Mount Ararat estate, used as allotments during the war.

52 Another aerial view taken by Captain Hutcheon in 1919, of Cottenham Park. It shows in the foreground Cambridge, Richmond, Durham, Lambton and Pepys Roads, with the war-time allotments beyond Pepys to the right. In the centre is Cottenham Park Road with the 1893 allotments on the left, Melbury Gardens in the middle and the future Holland Gardens (opened in 1929) to the right. Above lie the large houses lining Copse Hill, the Atkinson Morley and the Cottage Hospital. At the top, beyond Wimbledon Wood and the fairways of the Royal Wimbledon Golf course, are the tents of the Army Camp on the Common.

53 Copse Hill, looking towards Christ Church, late 1920s. The boys stand in the recently widened road, still quiet despite the opening of the Kingston by-pass in 1927. On the left are fields soon to be covered by Stiles's houses. On the right is the entrance to one of the large Italianate houses put up in the 1850s and recently converted into flats.

54 The wide expanse of the south part of Cottenham Park Road (by the present Old Wimbledonians' Rugby ground), April 1914. It was not made up until well after the Second World War. The small house, Wood Cottage (about where Oakwood Road is today), seems to have been a chicken farm with its free-range birds feeding on the road.

55 Durham Road, *c.*1910. These recently-built maisonettes, equipped with electric light and running hot and cold water, could be rented for £2.82 a month. On the field to the right of the road a unique type of aeroplane which flapped its wings, Mr. Passat's Ornithopter, was constructed in 1912. It crashed on its first and only flight on the Common.

56 Coombe Lane by Raynes Park station, *c.*1910. The *Raynes Park Hotel* had been opened shortly after the station was built in 1871 and had been enlarged in 1904. The parade of shops, then known as Amity Terrace, had been put up in the 1890s and are little changed today. The other side of the road has been transformed by the new station of 1935 and the cutting down of trees.

57 A tram travelling along Coombe Lane, *c.*1910. On the right is the bottom of Durham Road, with the trees on the left covering the site of the modern Metropolitan Water Board buildings. The land behind the two carts is now occupied by a line of shops, put up in the 1930s.

58 Coombe Lane near the junction with West Barnes Lane, *c*.1910. The road is narrow with a large drainage ditch behind railings on the right (where houses were not built until the early 1920s). The large late Victorian houses on the left are still there, though the trees in the background have gone.

59 Coombe Lane near the junction with Cambridge Road, *c*.1920. The Edwardian houses mostly survive. Behind the big drainage ditch and trees on the left are the fields of Hoppingwood Farm, once owned by the canons of Merton Priory and not developed until the later 1920s.

Part II: Aspects of Wimbledon

The Common

In the 1930s the Common was regarded proudly as part of our 'heritage' because it had been saved from enclosure and was ideal for 'exercise and recreation'. Yet in earlier centuries it had played a very different and even more important part in the lives of every householder. It had been 'the Common Waste', a large area of land whose soil was too poor for cultivation, but which provided pasture for animals and wood for the home. In theory it had been owned by the Lord of the Manor. In practice his tenants had 'rights of common' which were regulated by the Manor Court.

From early in the 18th century the Common had increasingly been used for sport—horse-racing, prize-fighting, even cricket. It had also become a haunt of highwaymen, until Jerry Abbershaw was caught and hung in 1795. Next it had been chosen as an ideal place for duels especially on the site of the modern Queensmere, where Lord Cardigan severely wounded Captain Tuckett in 1840. Above all, it had proved a perfect arena for large military reviews, especially by George III in the 1790s and by the German Kaiser, Wilhelm II, in 1891.

Just before the Kaiser's visit, between 1860 and 1889, the National Rifle Association had used the Common every July for a series of shooting competitions. The meetings attracted a large number of spectators and made Wimbledon famous. But in 1890 they had to be moved to Bisley as the rifles were becoming too powerful.

One of the keenest supporters of the N.R.A. was Wimbledon's Lord of the Manor, the fifth Earl Spencer. Attendance at the meetings made him realise the dreadful condition of the Common, with many swamps, piles of rubbish and 'gypsies, vagrants and trespassers'. He therefore proposed to turn the 700 acres south of the Portsmouth Road into a public park, surrounded by a low wall with new roads to make access easier. But his plan was bitterly opposed by the many professional men who had come to live in the new houses along Parkside and preferred 'an untamed Common to a manicured park'. In 1871 after a long legal battle the Earl agreed to a compromise. By the Wimbledon and Putney Commons Act he was guaranteed a yearly payment of £1,200 and in return handed over the area to a body of elected Conservators. Their duty was 'to keep the Commons open, unenclosed and unbuilt on' and to preserve them 'for the purpose of exercise and recreation'.

The Common soon changed dramatically. Grazing animals disappeared, trees and vegetation returned, and a new lake, known as Queensmere, was created to celebrate Queen Victoria's Golden Jubilee in 1887. Public meetings were also held at Rushmere, notably those of the Suffragettes.

60 The Windmill, *c*.1880. Built in 1817, it was an unusual 'hollow post' mill. The millers (who lived in the house on the left) also acted as constables to stop duels taking place nearby. In 1864 Earl Spencer took over the mill and converted it into six small cottages. By 1871 there were 19 people living in them without running water or a cooking range, but with a large kitchen garden.

61 Queensmere, *c*.1910. Once a large open piece of ground surrounded by trees and ideal for duels, it was transformed in 1887 into 'the Queen's Mere' to commemorate Victoria's Golden Jubilee.

62 The Pound in the snow, Parkside, *c.*1910. Originally situated in the High Street by the junction with Church Road, it was moved to its present position on the edge of the Common in the 18th century. It was used to keep animals which strayed when grazing, until claimed by their owners who had to pay a fine. In 1588 several horses were unclaimed and later sold.

63 The Old Gate House, Woodhayes Road, *c.*1905. It was one of several small cottages (others were in Church Road and the High Street) where elderly men looked after gates to stop cattle straying from the Common. In the early 19th century this one was known as 'Byde's Gate'. It did not disappear until the late 1920s when the land behind it was developed—as tennis courts and for the houses of Ernle Road. Opposite behind the fence are the grounds of Woodhayes House.

64 Drinking at Caesar's Well, *c*.1910. The well has nothing to do with Julius Caesar. It is the best known of the springs on the western edge of the Common and has been used since Neolithic times. In 1872 Sir Henry Peek, M.P. put up a circle of large granite blocks just to the north, but the water now comes from a standpipe which taps the spring 18 feet down. Its flow never stops, even in dry summers.

65 Mayes Farm, *c*.1905, with the Mayes children by the pond and their parents by the gate. Situated down Robin Hood ride to the west of Caesar's Camp, the farm seems to have been built in the 1860s. It was leased by the Mayes family who kept pigs, ducks and chickens, and later turned it into the Roman Well Laundry. The buildings were pulled down shortly after the Second World War.

66 The Council enclosure at the National Rifle Association meeting on the Common, July 1865, with the Windmill in the background and Manor Cottage, the official residence of the N.R.A., on the left. Every June and July between 1860 and 1889 the plateau around the Windmill was fenced in, a forest of tents and marquees set up and hundreds of riflemen arrived to compete for prizes.

67 Part of the N.R.A. camp, photographed from the Windmill, *c.*1885. In the centre is the Administrative Building. Beyond is the Umbrella Tent, the social centre, and on its left the Refreshment Pavilion. On the far right is the Clock Tower and an electric engine with carriages for spectators. In the foreground are the Windmill gardens and a number of tented shops.

68 N.R.A. short-range marksmen in the 1860s. They are aiming at butts just beyond Queensmere. Behind them are the Windmill and miller's house. To the right, behind the tents with one reserved for 'the Surgeon', is Manor Cottage.

69 The short-range N.R.A. targets on the other side of Queensmere, *c*.1870. Spectators and off-duty marksmen are watching the shooting behind a wooden barrier.

70 One of the N.R.A. butts across the Gulley (or Glen Albyn) to the south-west of the Windmill, *c*.1870.

71 The 158-foot flag-staff put up in 1871 to replace the original one destroyed by lightning. Made of Douglas pine, it remained a feature of the Common until 1928 when it became unsafe. The large Iron House beside it was used to store N.R.A. equipment.

72 'Volunteers entertaining at Wimbledon Camp', a watercolour by Sir John Gilbert, 1871. The N.R.A. summer meetings were great social occasions and made Wimbledon famous long before tennis did so. 'The shooting itself, except to experts', was said to be 'not particularly interesting'. But 'the refreshment department will supply everything a visitor can reasonably require'.

73 'A Wet Day at the Camp, July 1887' by Colonel J. Bland. N.R.A. meetings were as much at the mercy of the weather as are the Tennis Championships today.

74 Kaiser Wilhelm II riding up Wimbledon Hill to review the British Army on the Common, July 1891. With him are his nephews, Edward Prince of Wales on his left and Arthur Duke of Connaught on his right. On the Common the line of red-coated soldiers extended from the Windmill to near Rushmere. The Emperor was said to have been 'greatly impressed' by this last great military review on the Common.

75 Curling on the Common in the late 19th century. One of the sports introduced by the London Scottish Regiment, it was normally played on a specially flooded curling rink in Camp Road. But this rink seems to have been made on one of the old gravel pits above North View.

76 Rushmere Pond in 1908. Known as 'Rushmore' in Tudor times, it was a source of the rushes used in cottages and an ideal place for the villagers' ducks. By Edwardian times rushes and ducks had been replaced by mothers, nannies and their charges out for a walk. In the background is the Green, with newly built houses to the left and Holly Cottage, the white building to right of centre.

77 A Suffragette meeting on the Common, 1913. The speaker is Mrs. Rose Lamartine Yates of Dorset Hall, Merton, a leading member of the militant W.S.P.U. (Women's Social and Political Union). Behind her stand her two lady supporters and her husband. Despite the presence of the police, these meetings were often broken up and the speakers attacked, but Mrs. Yates carried on Sunday after Sunday.

78 West Place, 1892. In the background are old cottages and a tall ivy-clad house, the Hermitage, where the prolific Victorian novelist, Margaret Oliphant, died in 1897. On the Common a small flock of sheep are returning home; poles are ready to support clothes lines to dry the washing from the laundries behind the cottages; and on the left are piles of timber to be cut up in a saw-pit.

79 No. 26 West Place, 1906. Edwin Hill, a builder and decorator, and his wife and daughters stand in front of their home, while their workmen hold the firm's cart. Behind the pony and trap is a builder's yard where fencing used at N.R.A. meetings had been stored.

The Churches

Like the Common, the parish church of St Mary the Virgin has played an essential part in the lives of the people of Wimbledon. For around 1,000 years through all the disruption caused by events like the Norman Conquest, the Black Death, the Reformation and the Civil War, its parsons have ministered to their spiritual needs. Until 1859 it was the only church in the village and so was the place where Sunday after Sunday the inhabitants went to morning service. Many were christened and married there; many too were ultimately buried in the churchyard.

Before the Reformation they were served by wealthy rectors like Walter Reynolds (1298-1309) who were often absentees. For two centuries afterwards services were conducted by badly paid vicars like Edward Collins (1684-1739) who were regarded by the Lord of the Manor as 'household chaplains'. Since then the parsons have been more independent, some like Henry Haygarth (1859-1902) highly respected personalities. It was while he was vicar that the population dramatically increased. The Anglican response was to build 10 new churches in Wimbledon. Yet by 1900 (as in 1850) rarely more than a third of the population were attending their services. The hold of the Established Church on the old parish had clearly come to an end.

Few Nonconformists had lived in Wimbledon before the 1840s. But many of the new residents, if they came to church at all, were more attracted by their services. Consequently from the 1860s there was a big increase in the numbers of Baptists, Congregationalists, Methodists and Presbyterians. They all built large churches and together by 1903 drew more people on Sundays than the Church of England.

Equally successful were the Roman Catholics. Before 1877 their numbers in Wimbledon had been tiny. But then a Mass centre was opened in Cottenham Park at the home of a wealthy convert, Edith Arendrup. The congregation grew so fast that in 1887 a large new church was built on Edge Hill, followed by a second in South Wimbledon. Both were in the charge of Jesuit priests who attracted such large numbers that their parishes were soon among the most flourishing in the Roman Catholic Church south of the Thames.

After the First World War, however, the habit of church-going declined. Only one new church was built in the borough, the Roman Catholic Christ the King in Wimbledon Park. Nonetheless the different denominations did their best to help the unemployed in the 1930s. Anglicans at Holy Trinity in the Broadway paid them to clean and paint their church, while the nearby Methodists allowed them to use their hall for 'rest and recreation'.

80 'Wimbledon church on a Monday morning'. The medieval St Mary's, painted *c.*1780 by John Barralet. The small parish church had a nave just capable of holding everyone in the village, a chancel rarely used after the Reformation and a mortuary chapel for the Cecil family. The watercolour shows the end of a tithe barn on the left and the parson (probably Herbert Randolph) behind the wall.

81 The Georgian St Mary's, a print of 1809. Built 20 years earlier after the medieval nave had become too small for the rapidly growing population, its copper spire was paid for by the Prime Minister, William Pitt, who attended services on his frequent visits to Wimbledon. The medieval chancel was retained, along with the Cecil chapel (to the right behind the main body of the church).

82 The Victorian St Mary's, designed by Sir George Gilbert Scott in 1841 and photographed in 1862. The nave was again enlarged, but it was still too small and extra Anglican churches had to be built. The tithe barn on the left was dismantled in 1864 to enlarge the churchyard.

83 Canon James Bell, vicar of St Mary's 1903-1918, and his nine curates, c.1910. They served five churches in Wimbledon. Today four of these churches are served by a rector and two team vicars.

84 The Baptist Church, Queens Road, in 1988 just before it was pulled down to make way for the Centre Court shopping mall. It had been built in 1897 to seat a congregation of 1,000 who came every Sunday to hear the eloquent sermons of Rev. Charles Ingrem. In its place the Baptists have been given a new church nearby.

85 The South Wimbledon Methodist church to the left of the tram, *c.*1910. Before the First World War Methodists were strong in Wimbledon, with two large churches in Worple Road. Since 1945 support has dropped, one church in Worple Road has been pulled down and this church in Merton Road (built in 1904) has been completely reconstructed.

86 The Methodist Central Hall, Durnsford Road, Wimbledon Park, *c*.1980. Built in 1924, it had room for a congregation of 1,500 and so was easily the largest church in the area. It was said to have been 'equipped for talking pictures'. With the congregation declining, it has recently been pulled down and replaced by a much smaller, modern church.

87 Barkby Close, Cottenham Park Road, 1993. Built in 1876, it was the home of Edith Arendrup, a Roman Catholic convert. She built a small chapel onto the house, where Mass was said for the few Catholics in the area. Within 10 years the congregation had grown so fast that she had the Sacred Heart church built. The house and chapel are now threatened with development.

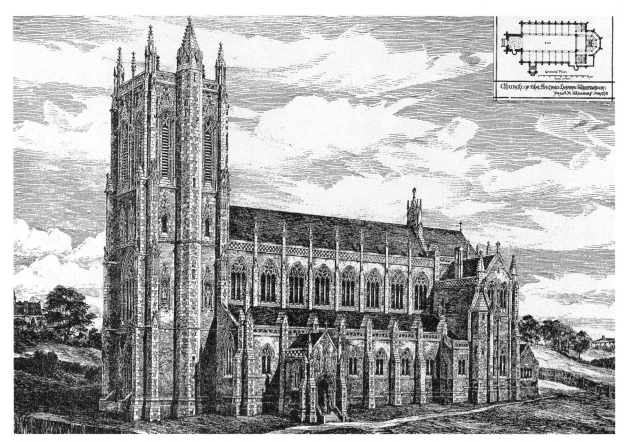

Church of the Sacred Heart, Wimbledon.

88 Frederick Walters's original design for the Sacred Heart church, 1886. It shows rather a different building from the one completed in 1901. The nave and aisles are very much the same, but the chancel is much smaller and there is a magnificent tower at the west end.

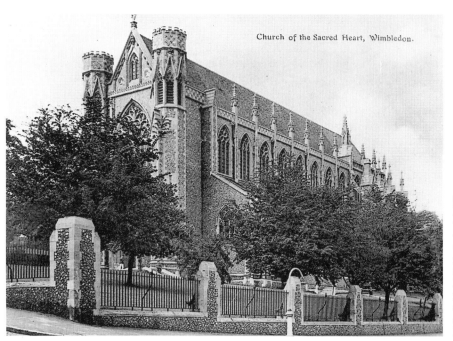

89 The Sacred Heart church, Edge Hill, 1922. Instead of a tower, the church was completed with twin turrets and a large west window. Even without the tower, it is one of the finest Roman Catholic churches in South London. The railings disappeared in 1940. In the foreground is one of the 'filling stations' for water carts, used between the Wars to keep dust down in dry summers.

Schools

Wimbledon had only one church before 1859, but until the early 18th century it did not have a single school. The parson sometimes taught poorer children to read and write, while wealthy parents sent their sons away to school or, like William Cecil, employed a tutor. Sons of the richer farmers, such as Robert Bell, went to London to train as apprentices.

In the 1720s, however, two small charity schools were set up, but did not last long. Then in 1758 a new charity school was built on the Common, yet within ten years it too had collapsed for lack of money. In 1773 it was refounded on a much sounder basis and from then until after the Second World War provided a good basic education for many local boys and girls.

Once Wimbledon began to grow fast in the 1860s, other 'elementary schools for the benefit of the labouring classes' were set up by the Church of England in new districts like Haydons Road and Cottenham Park. Evening schools to help youths out at work were also founded by the clergy, who then provided domestic service courses for girls. This Anglican monopoly was resented by Nonconformists who campaigned for non-sectarian or Board schools after the Education Act of 1871. Until 1905, however, the primary schools continued under parish control and parents had to pay a penny a week towards their children's education.

Meantime many private schools for middle-class children had been set up. The first for boys was started in 1790 at Eagle House in the High Street by a clergyman, Rev. Thomas Lancaster. Under a variety of headmasters it flourished for nearly a hundred years. Girls had to wait until 1830 when a Mrs. Terry founded a 'Ladies' Boarding School' in Church Road. But the real expansion only started in 1879 with the founding of a small preparatory school named Rokeby, soon followed by the High School (1880), Hazelhurst (1882), Wimbledon College (1892), the Ursuline Convent (1892) and the Study (1893). While other private schools foundered, all these prospered and have now celebrated their centenaries. Kings College School moved to Wimbledon from the Strand in 1897 and commissioned a leading architect, Sir Banister Fletcher, to design a new assembly hall.

In the present century the borough has prided itself on schools whose reputation 'extends well beyond its boundaries'. One of the most notable was the Wimbledon School of Art which was given large new buildings in 1940 just before the Battle of Britain.

90 'Charity School on Wimbledon Common. Sketched 9 July 1810 by William Porden.' Put up in 1758, the octagonal building in Camp Road continued in use for 200 years as a 'National School' or 'The Old Central'. It has recently been adapted for handicapped children.

91 'The Revd Mr Lancaster's Academy, Wimbledon', drawn in 1810 by the art master, R.B. Schnebbelie. Opened 20 years earlier in Eagle House, High Street, the school gave about sixty boys aged between six and 16 a reasonable education. The most famous pupil, Arthur Schopen-hauer, the German philosopher, was there for three months in 1803—and hated it.

The Revd Mr Lancasters Academy · Wimbledon.

EAGLE HOUSE,

WIMBLEDON, SURREY, S.W.

—⁂—

Pupils, from the age of Eight to Fifteen, are prepared for Eton, Winchester, Harrow, Rugby, and other Public Schools.

Those pupils usually succeed best at Public Schools, who are sent to Eagle House at Nine and remain until they have been at least a full year in the First Class.

MASTERS.

THE REV. E. HUNTINGFORD, D.C.L.,
Late Fellow of New College, Oxford.
⎱ PRINCIPALS.
MR. A. N. MALAN,
Oriel College, Oxford.

THE REV. O. C. CHAMBERLAIN, *Worcester College, Oxford.*

MR. W. J. EGAR, *Christ's College, Cambridge.*

MR. R. WALTHAM, *St. Peter's College, Cambridge.*

MR. E. LEIGH BENNETT, *Corpus Christi College, Oxford.*

MONS. BRUN,
HERR PONSSEN, ⎱ Non-Resident Masters.

Terms:

Board, Washing, and Instruction in Greek, Latin, French, English, Mathematics, Arithmetic, History, Geography, Physical Science, Drilling, Gymnastics, and Vocal Music when desirable:

NINETY GUINEAS PER ANNUM.

Pupils intended for the Modern Side at any Public School, or who are not intended to compete for admission on the Foundation at Eton or Winchester, or for any open Scholarship, may, at the wish of their Parents, be excused Latin verses and be taught German instead on the above terms.

EXTRA SUBJECTS WHEN REQUIRED.

	Per Annum.
Drawing	£5 5 0
Instrumental Music	8 8 0
Dancing	5 5 0
Riding—Two Guineas for a dozen lessons.	

A Term's Notice or payment is required before the removal of any Pupil from the School, and no deductions are made for occasional absence.

☞ To prevent delay and inconvenience, it is particularly requested that every boy should bring with him, when he comes back to School, a small bag or parcel containing the things required for the night.

[TURN OVER.

92 Prospectus of Eagle House School, 1865. Five years earlier a new Headmaster, Dr. Huntingford, had brought a stone eagle, which he fixed to the central gable. His school proved so successful that in 1886 it moved to Camberley, where it recently celebrated its centenary.

93 The Study, Peek Crescent, 1906, three years after the school had moved there. It had been started in 1893 when two teachers combined their groups of senior girls and set up a school in a converted shop, 47 High Street. This picture of the fine new building shows that the school was growing with classes for young, as well as senior, girls.

94 Girls from the Study by Margin Lake, *c*.1907. The artificial lake, created in the 1770s in the grounds of Wimbledon House Parkside, had just become part of the estate of Arthur Wills, the cigarette manufacturer, who built Margin House, Marryat Road. In the 1960s the lake was drained and houses built along Margin Drive.

95 A junior class at the Study, *c*.1903, with two of their mistresses.

96 The entrance to Wimbledon College, Edge Hill, *c*.1905. The buildings were designed by Samuel Teulon in 1860 for an Army crammers, Wimbledon School, run by Rev. J.M. Brackenbury. In 1892 they were bought by the Jesuit Fathers who had just opened a Roman Catholic College in Darlaston Road. The ivy-clad hall was burnt down in 1977.

97 The front of King's College School, Southside, *c*.1905. The school, set up in the Strand in 1831, moved in 1897 to South Hayes, an 18th-century house facing the Common with eight acres of ground. It has since become one of the country's leading public schools.

98 An aerial view of Ridgways School, 1950s. Built as a private house in the 1860s, it was opened as a girls' school, Oakhill, in 1930. Among the pupils were Dorothy Tutin and Pat Smythe. Closed at the start of the Second World War, it was later reopened as Ridgways Coeducational School and flourished until it suddenly folded in the late 1950s. Ten years later the buildings were pulled down and a group of town houses and maisonettes built on the site.

99 A Raynes Park Elementary School class, 1929-30. Thirty-five small boys and girls with their teacher in a sparsely-furnished classroom. But just above the E in the left corner is a railway track brought by one of the boys.

Shops

One result of Wimbledon's growing prosperity after the building of the Elizabethan manor house was the opening in the High Street of the first shops. In the 1550s a baker had been fined for 'baking underweight bread' and at the time of the Armada a 'scissor' or tailor had lived in Church Road. But there is no sign that either sold their goods in a shop. At the time of the Civil War, however, a butcher, Phanuel Maybank, arrived from Kingston, established himself in what was clearly a shop and prospered. In the next fifty years his example was followed by a barber, a 'cordwainer' (shoemaker), a 'cheesemonger', a haberdasher, a button-seller, a confectioner and a grocer.

The exact position of the shops can first be seen on the Spencer map of the village in 1776. On the western side of the High Street there was a tailor, glazier and plumber, a butcher and baker, and round the corner by Claremont House a general store which sold a wide variety of goods from butter and sugar to snuff, clogs and candles. Up Church Road there was a line of small shops on the northern side, including two barbers.

Until the late 1850s there were no shops anywhere else in Wimbledon. Then 'The Terrace' was built at the southern end of the High Street opposite the top of the Hill; among the original shops was a baker's which is still selling bread. Twenty years later the first shops appeared in the Broadway; their name and date, 'Prospect Terrace 1876' can be seen near the modern Woolworth's. By the 1890s there was also a line of shops opposite the library, including Russell and Sons, 'photographers to the Queen', and round the corner a collection of small shops where Sainsbury's is today. Already Cottenham Park had 'Commercial Place' and 'Market Place' in Durham Road, as well as Amity and Raynes Park Terraces opposite the station.

Without supermarkets to threaten their livelihood, traders competed for business by advertising their attention to customers: 'Families waited upon daily'; 'Highly recommended by several doctors of the parish'; 'van and barrows deliver all through Wimbledon and Merton'; 'orders executed by prompt and experienced workmen'. The official guide could justly claim that local shops had 'an enviable reputation for good service'. By the 1970s there were over 700 of them, an amazing growth in just a hundred years.

100 'H.J. and W. Hudnott. General Smiths, Hot-Water Engineers, Gas Fitters etc. Established 1814', Crooked Billet, 1913. The first Henry Hudnott had set up his business here as a blacksmith and farrier just before the Battle of Waterloo. His descendants were still in business at the start of the Second World War. Beyond is the *Crooked Billet* public house.

101 Siggers and Son, Boot-makers, 61 High Street, 1926. According to an advertisement of 1900 they made 'ladies, gentlemen's and children's boots and shoes of every description to order (under their personal superintendence)' and 'waited upon families at their own residences'. The last Mr. Siggers sold the shop and retired in 1928.

102 Lemuel Brooks, Saddler and Harness-maker, 26 Hartfield Road, 1911. 'Established 1870', as its sign-board proudly proclaims, Brooks must be Wimbledon's oldest surviving shop on its original site. Though now dealing mostly in suitcases, umbrellas and leather goods, it is still in the same building dating from the early years of New Wimbledon.

103 Ely's corner, *c*.1905, before the arrival of the trams. Joseph Ely, 'tailor, outfitter and draper', opened his first shop on the corner of Alexandra Road in 1876. Ten years later he built a second, much larger shop at the corner of Worple Road over the front gardens of two earlier houses where he and his family lived. Opposite is the studio of James Russell, the photographer, with Russell himself in a hat standing on the balcony.

104 W. Hughes and Co., General Ironmongers, 1 Hartfield Road, *c*.1900. Starting in 1876 in Tooting with a capital of £30, Walter Hughes moved to Wimbledon four years later. The shop became famous for its wonderful assortment of goods. It had to close in 1986 after the site was compulsorily purchased by the Council for the building of hideous modern offices.

105 Johnston's advertisement, 'How to create employment', 1926. A.J. Johnston, son of an Edinburgh baker, came to Wimbledon in 1886 and opened a baker's shop in the newly built Bank Buildings in Hill Road. He then set up a machine bakery in Mansel Road, as well as a popular restaurant and two more shops, in the Broadway and High Street.

HOW TO CREATE EMPLOYMENT

1. Eat more Bread and help the agricultural labourer.

2. Lunch in our Restaurants and reduce the quantity of Imported Food.

3. 2d. more per customer per week, spent in our shops, will employ one Sales-woman and one Baker.

4. The more you entertain your friends the more staff will be required to carry out the catering.

5. An extra slice of Bread per day will create employment for one Baker.

JOHNSTONS

39-41 HILL ROAD; 58-59 HIGH STREET; and opposite the Town Hall.

Telephone Nos.: Wimbledon 0833-34-35

106 Berkshire Dairy, 31 High Street, 1913, one of over 30 dairies in Wimbledon before the First World War. The Berkshires had been poor labourers living near the Common since the 1760s. But about 1890 Thomas Berkshire leased Broadwater Farm, Cannon Hill Lane. His large herd of cows provided 'pure new milk' until the early 1920s when the farm was sold for development and the family emigrated to Texas.

107 One of the Berkshire milkmen, Mr. Brown, 1898. He delivered milk from his 'chariot' with its large churn to houses in West Place, North View, Camp Road and Westside. His hours were very long—4 a.m. to 3 p.m.—and he had to make several deliveries a day as homes then did not have refrigerators.

108 An alternative means of delivery—a Berkshire hand-cart with some of the early milk bottles. The date of the photo is unknown, but it must have been in the 1920s as the poster advertises films at the Rialto cinema, Raynes Park.

109 Jefferys Fishshop, Durham Road, Cottenham Park, in the early 1920s. George Jefferys, standing by the door with his wife and young son (who still runs the shop), came from Southend in 1900 and established a very successful fish shop. The prices for his wide variety of fish, as well as 'English Rabbits', can be seen marked on the board.

110 George Jefferys with his daughters sitting in the cart from which he made his rounds, taking orders and delivering fish to his customers.

111 'Wimbledon Park Engineering Works', *c.*1920. Messrs. Bachelier and Hawkins Motor Repair shop, 74 Arthur Road, displays some of the latest 'tyres and accessories', as well as bicycles and motorcycles with side-cars. The building is now part of an enlarged Barclays Bank.

Transport

Before the present century most Wimbledonians were used to walking quite long distances. Farmers had a horse and cart to get them to market. Gentlemen owned not merely several horses, but often their own coach to take them to and from London. Ordinary people, however, had no means of public transport. The village was not on one of the main roads. It could only attract a coach if a sufficient number wanted to travel regularly.

By 1790 enough did. A short-stage coach to London left from the *Rose and Crown* and took two hours for the journey to Charing Cross. By the 1820s demand had grown and a second coach set off from the *Dog and Fox*. But poorer people could not afford the fare and most of the passengers were professional men who worked in the City.

A transport revolution was foreshadowed in 1838 when the London and South-Western Railway opened a station at the bottom of the hill. The trains only took 18 minutes to reach the first terminus at Nine Elms, but barely three thousand people used the station in the summer of 1845. Once Wimbledon became a junction in the 1860s, however, and the station was rebuilt, professional men began to travel regularly to work by train, even though the carriages were said to be 'rather decrepit'.

It was the aptly named omnibus that first enticed ordinary people to travel to work. The first one reached Wimbledon in the early 1850s. It ran from the City twice a day via Knightsbridge and Putney and had the advantage of lower fares, though (like the short-stage) it took about two hours for the journey. By the 1880s there was a horse bus to Putney. Twenty years later the Tilling Company introduced the first motor buses with solid rubber tyres.

Just as these new buses appeared, cheaper travel for everyone became a reality. After major alterations to local roads (especially Worple Road), a tram service between Tooting and Hampton Court was started in 1907. It was much better and cheaper than trains or buses, especially for workmen who could travel to London in an hour for two pence.

Meantime life for many richer Wimbledonians had been transformed by two new inventions. First in the 1890s came the 'safety' bicycle and the formation of cycle clubs which went 'along the empty, dusty roads to such places as Ewell, Ripley and Epsom'. Then ten years later the first motor cars appeared in Wimbledon. They were greeted at the top of the Hill by a large notice: 'Caution. Hill. Dangerous. Speed Limit. Motors requested 10 Miles per hour.' By the start of the First World War there were enough cars on the road to justify seven garages in the borough, but still most of the traffic passing along the Ridgway could be described as 'horse-drawn, hand-pushed or foot-pedalled'. The car really came into its own in 1927 with the opening of the Kingston by-pass.

112 The unusual sight of a stage coach rounding the corner of the High Street, *c.*1900. It would have been on a special run, perhaps to the Derby. In the background is the fine fire brigade engine house, built in 1890, with its high telephone pole. To the right are two famous High Street shops. At the junction with Church Road is a lamp-standard, used also as a 'finger-post'.

113 A horse-bus from Putney in the southern part of the High Street, *c.*1908. The western side of the road is already lined with shops, most still there today. But the other side has only begun to be developed with the surviving trees of Belvedere House garden extending over the road. The shops here were not built until 1924.

114 The Malcolm carriage outside 'Canisbay', 3 Southside, 1892. Two members of the family wait at the front door. The open carriage with a hood for bad weather would be used for social calls or visits to London. So a coachman like Rogers was essential for a Victorian upper-class family.

115 A biking party, 1900. Two of the Malcolm girls, Elizabeth (fourth from the left) and Kittie (second from the right), posing with their friends on the latest 'safety' bicycles which were very popular in the years around 1900.

116 A steam train on the main line passing the Durnsford Road Power Station, *c*.1920. The local lines had been electrified in 1915. Some of the first electric trains can be seen on the left of the picture. The power station had been built in 1899.

117 'The 10 a.m. up': Commuters waiting on Wimbledon station for a steam train to London, *c*.1910.

118 The approach to the station, *c.*1910. The booking-office for Waterloo is on the right; that for the District Line is in the background to the left. Horse-drawn cabs or 'flys' wait outside both exits. Their drivers have a small corrugated shelter on the left in front of a large poster advertising the week's films at the King's Palace. On the far left are coal offices and Hawes furniture depository.

119 The station, *c.*1920, with early motor-cars waiting outside both exits. The railway bridge on the right led to the platforms and the exit near the Town Hall.

120 Tracks being laid for the trams on Wimbledon Bridge, 1906. The station is to the right with the waiting cabs outside. On the left of Hill Road are a number of small shops added on to the original houses built in the 1870s.

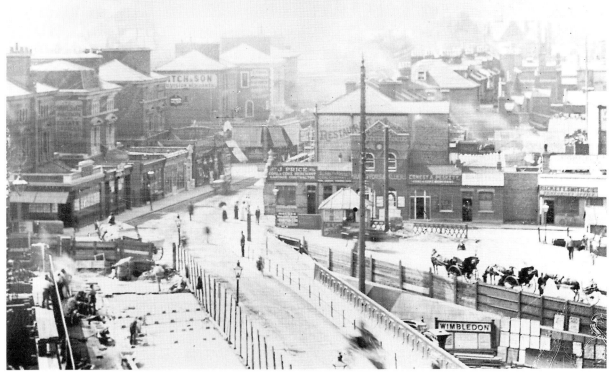

121 A cartoon on the long delayed arrival of the first tram in Hill Road, 2 May 1907. The London United Tramways Company had been given the right to extend its line at Tooting to Wimbledon and Hampton Court in 1902. But it took five years to widen the roads and lay the tracks. Hence the banners in the cartoon and the reaction of both horses and pedestrians.

122 Jack the trace-horse helping to pull a wood-cart up Wimbledon Hill in the 1920s. For 30 years from 1908 a series of powerful horses, all known as Jack, made about 20 journeys a day from a box at the bottom of the hill. The increasing use of lorries in the 1930s led to the last horse being pensioned off just before the start of the Second World War.

123 A motor bus to Putney Bridge going up Wimbledon Hill, *c*.1920. It had replaced the old horse buses just before the First World War.

124 Mr. Hall in front of his new charabanc in Durnsford Road, 1924. This early form of motor coach with its long running-board, individual doors for each seat and large hood for bad weather was very popular in the 1920s for excursions. W.D. Hall Coaches was still in business after the Second World War.

125 A tram and trolley-bus waiting outside the Town Hall in the 1930s. Trolley-buses replaced trams on the service to Kingston and Hampton Court in 1931. Trams now began their journeys to Tooting and the Embankment here. They continued to operate until 1951, the year when the trollies were themselves replaced by buses.

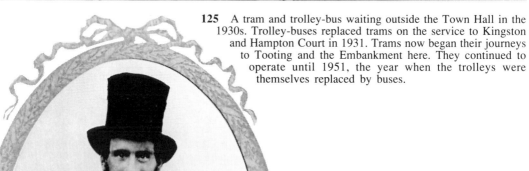

126 Samuel Syritt, Wimbledon's postman, c.1858. Before starting his rounds, he had to walk to Putney to collect the mail, as there was no official Post Office in the village until 1879. This photograph is one of the earliest in the Wimbledon Society's collection.

Local Government

Except at times of crisis or bitter controversy, local government has aroused little interest in Wimbledon. Most people have been far more concerned with the problems of daily life and have left politics to a minority of enthusiasts.

The Vestry, a parish parliament which discussed and controlled local affairs from the reign of Elizabeth I, was open to every rate-payer. But, though the meetings were often held in the parlours of local inns, rarely more than twenty men (mostly farmers and shop-keepers) attended. Their chief concern (apart from law and order, and keeping the roads in repair) was to raise the money needed to provide relief for the ever-growing number of poor people.

In 1866 the growth of New Wimbledon led to the setting up of a Local Board of Health. Originally dealing just with sanitation and infectious diseases, it was soon given extra powers: to control the building of new houses and roads, the water supply, the fire brigade and a public library (set up in 1887). Its members, elected by rate-payers, employed a growing number of paid officials. So in 1878 they bought land just below the station and built the first Local Board Offices.

In 1895 the Board was transformed by Parliament into an Urban District Council. It used the same offices and the same officials, but its members were chosen by a wider number of householders. They promptly tried to have Wimbledon made a borough with its own charter, which would give them greater power to improve the town. But they failed to convince a majority of the voters until 1904. The following year the new charter was approved by the King and brought to Wimbledon through cheering crowds by the first Mayor, Alderman Hamshaw.

A Borough Council ran Wimbledon affairs from 1905 to 1965. It consisted of a Mayor, eight Aldermen and 24 Councillors, elected by those with a right to vote in national elections. For the whole 60 years of its existence it was controlled by Conservatives. They improved the roads, the welfare services and the water supply, as well as building a new Town Hall (opened in 1931) in an attempt 'to make Wimbledon an even better place to live in'. But they were criticised for their poor housing record and for their inability to help the unemployed during the slump in the 1930s.

So the Charter Jubilee in 1955 aroused little interest and ten years later there were relatively few protests at the ending of Wimbledon's long tradition of local government until it was too late.

127 A portrait of Thomas Watney (1785-1867), grandson of Daniel Watney, founder of the famous family, and a leading member of the Vestry in the 1820s. He lived at Rushmere House, Southside, and farmed an estate of about 100 acres. He seems to have been the last member of his family to live in Wimbledon.

128 The first Town Hall, *c.*1914. Built in 1878 as offices for the Local Board of Health, it became a Town Hall when Wimbledon gained its Borough Charter in 1905. It soon became too small for the growing responsibilities of the Council, but was not replaced by a new Town Hall until 1931. On the right of the picture a cart horse drinks from the trough. To the left of the Town Hall are the Municipal Offices and a side entrance to the station.

129 Charter Day, 26 July 1905. The Borough Charter was greeted by huge crowds at the Merton boundary and taken in procession to the Town Hall, where it was read to an assembly of distinguished guests, including the Lord Mayor of London, the Lord-Lieutenant of Surrey, local M.P.s and Mayors.

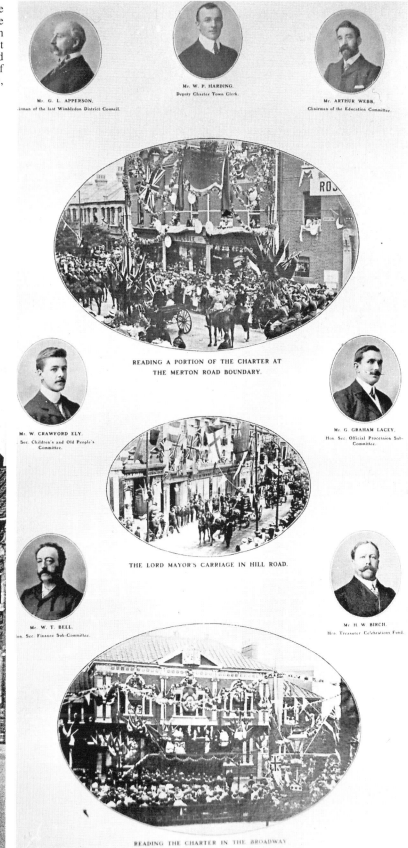

Mr. G. L. APPERSON.
Chairman of the last Wimbledon District Council.

Mr. W. P. HARDING.
Deputy Charter Town Clerk.

Mr. ARTHUR WEBB.
Chairman of the Education Committee.

READING A PORTION OF THE CHARTER AT THE MERTON ROAD BOUNDARY.

Mr. W. CRAWFORD ELY.
Sec. Children's and Old People's Committee.

Mr. G. GRAHAM LACEY.
Hon. Sec. Official Procession Sub-Committee.

THE LORD MAYOR'S CARRIAGE IN HILL ROAD.

Mr. W. T. BELL.
Hon. Sec. Finance Sub-Committee.

Mr. H. W. BIRCH.
Hon. Treasurer Celebrations Fund.

READING THE CHARTER IN THE BROADWAY

130 The Charter celebrations at King's College School: the new Mayor, Councillors and guests after a large lunch in the hall and a long selection of speeches. At the same time the people of Wimbledon were being entertained on the Common by 'a Grand Military Display and Tournament', a Carnival Procession and at nightfall a huge bonfire accompanied by fireworks.

131 Wimbledon Council and its chief officers, 1923. The Mayor, Mr. Pauling, and his wife sit in the middle with the Town Clerk, H. Emerson-Smith. Previous Mayors sit on Pauling's right: first Alderman Bathgate (1909-11, 1931), then Alderman Stuart (1919-21) and Alderman Mussell (1921-3). In the next row stand later Mayors: behind Bathgate and Stuart, Councillor Ramshaw (1931-3), behind the Mayor, Lady Roney (1933-5), next to her Councillor Drake (1941-3), just behind him to the right Councillor Hickmott (1926-8) and finally the second Councillor further right Mullins (1937-8).

132 Banky Field, Wimbledon Park, 1927. This 'beautiful, wooded and sloping ground' on the south side of Home Park Road was bought by the Council in 1914 along with the rest of the Park. Eleven years later the Council announced that it was to be sold for building. There were violent protests and a public enquiry. The Council won their case: the Field was developed, but the Mayor, Alderman Hickmott, lost his seat at the next election.

133   The two steam fire-engines and hose cart at Wimbledon House Parkside, 1894. The volunteer firemen look as if they have just given a demonstration of fire-fighting at the empty home of Sir Henry Peek, M.P., who had recently retired to Devon. Only six years later they were unable to deal with a genuine fire at Cannizaro on the opposite side of the Common.

134 Parade of the Wimbledon fire brigade, 18 July 1900. Two steam fire-engines, followed by the hose cart and a manual engine lead a two-mile Carnival procession of floats with two military bands. Their aim, to raise money to help the families of soldiers fighting in South Africa, was rewarded with a sum of £224. The front engine is by Elys corner.

135 The fire station, Queens Road, *c*.1910. For the past three years all the engines had been kept here, manned by full-time, paid firemen. The pair of greys in the picture had been trained to slip their heads into their collars as soon as the alarm bell rang. But in 1913 they were replaced by motors.

136 An individual invitation to Coronation dinner, held at St Mark's church hall near the public library, 26 June 1902. The dinner, given by the Council for 'the aged poor' who were over sixty years old, went ahead, although two days earlier the coronation had hurriedly to be postponed after Edward VII had an emergency operation. He was finally crowned six weeks later.

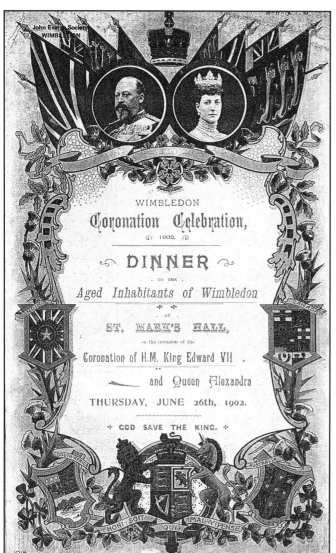

WIMBLEDON
Coronation Celebration,
1902

~ DINNER ~

. TO THE .

Aged Inhabitants of Wimbledon

AT

ST. MARK'S HALL,

on the occasion of the

Coronation of H.M. King Edward VII

and *Queen Alexandra*

THURSDAY, JUNE 26th, 1902.

+ GOD SAVE THE KING. +

137 Invitation to an 'Electrical Exhibition', November 1909. The exhibition—of the latest electric fires—was promoted by the Council which in 1899 had commissioned Arthur Preece to design a power station in Durnsford Road. By 1909 Wimbledon's streets were lit by electricity instead of by oil lamps and over 3,000 homes were using electric power.

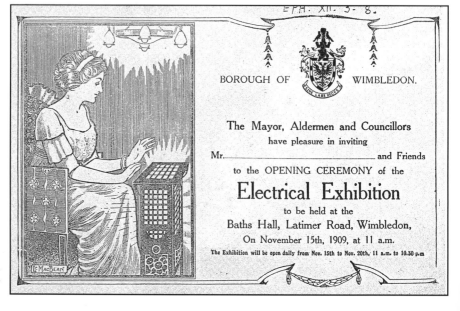

BOROUGH OF WIMBLEDON.

The Mayor, Aldermen and Councillors

have pleasure in inviting

Mr... and Friends

to the OPENING CEREMONY of the

Electrical Exhibition

to be held at the

Baths Hall, Latimer Road, Wimbledon,

On November 15th, 1909, at 11 a.m.

The Exhibition will be open daily from Nov. 15th to Nov. 20th, 11 a.m. to 10.30 p.m

138 The opening of *Draxmont Hotel*, Wimbledon Hill, 8 June 1922. Guests listen respectfully to a speech by Lady Cooper. Among them are the Mayor, Alderman Mussell and his wife, seated on the right, and the Vicar of Wimbledon, Canon Monroe, standing just behind the other seated lady. The hotel was pulled down in the 1970s and replaced by a large block of flats.

139 The public library, Compton Road, *c*.1922. Opened in 1887 after a long debate on whether a free library was really needed, it soon proved its value as one in twelve of the adult population enrolled as members in the first year. So in 1901 new lending and reference sections (to the left of the picture) were added, designed by Robert Thomson. The railings disappeared in 1940.

Free Library, Wimbledon.

140 The Civic Hall, 1989. Like the Town Hall, it was designed by A.J. Hope and opened in 1931. It became the centre for music and drama festivals, school prize-givings and a variety of entertainments. Despite strong public protests, it was pulled down by Merton Council in 1989 to make way for the Centre Court shopping mall and has not been replaced.

141 The Council Chamber in the second Town Hall, photographed from the public gallery in 1989. The Wimbledon Council debates were held here from 1931 to 1965, with the Mayor presiding from his official chair. For just over 20 years it was also used by the Merton Council, until the move to Crown House, Morden. It is now waiting to be transformed into a restaurant.

Leisure

Little is known of how local farmers, tradesmen and labourers spent their leisure before Victorian times. Many clearly relaxed at one of the local pubs—the oldest, the *Dog and Fox*. There they could forget their worries, play at cards and dice (both strictly illegal) or join in a game of bowls on a green at the back. There is evidence that a number enjoyed poaching with 'nets, ferrets and hare-hounds'. Many more seem to have enjoyed the fair which took place in the High Street on the first Monday after Easter—until it was suppressed by the Vestry in 1840 on the grounds that it was 'disorderly' and had 'a bad moral effect on the people'. Many, too, watched prize-fights or military reviews on the Common in the reign of George III. But neither football nor cock-fighting are mentioned in any local document and there is little sign of any interest in reading, except in the autobiography of a seaman, Robert Knox. Brought up in Wimbledon at the time of the Civil War, he remembered that, while his mother and sister were knitting or sewing, he was 'set to read by them in the Bible or some other godly book'.

Until the 18th century books rarely appeared among the possessions even of wealthy Wimbledonians. General Lambert was the first Lord of the Manor to have 'a scholar's library' and his example was followed by Sir Theodore Janssen. But the greatest readers were the Spencer family. Their 'usual evening occupation' was reading, unless they had visitors when they played cards, 'cribbage, whist or Pope Joan', often for money. They also enjoyed musical evenings, playing the piano or singing glees.

The arrival of professional middle-class families after 1850 led to a more earnest, organised use of leisure. In 1859 some of them founded the Village Club on the Ridgway and provided a reading room and a large hall where lectures were given every fortnight. Other clubs were founded to promote sport: cricket (1854), golf (1865), rugby (1869), croquet (1869), followed by lawn tennis (1875), hockey (1883) and football (1889). Most clubs played their games on the Common until Wimbledon Park became available for sport in the 1890s.

Many other clubs and societies were started in the final decades of Queen Victoria's reign: a Choral Society, cycling clubs, a Poultry Club, an Arts and Drama Society and many others. Their meetings were all recorded in the first local papers, especially *The Surrey Independent* (1876-1905) and *The Wimbledon News* (1894-1993).

An even more dramatic change in leisure habits began in 1909 when the first 'Electric Theatre' (later the Queen's Cinema) opened in the Worple Hall. Competition soon came, not merely from the rival King's Palace, but from its neighbour, Wimbledon Theatre, whose first productions, including a pantomime, *Jack and Jill*, were soon attracting 'packed houses'. An age of mass entertainment had begun.

142   The *Dog and Fox* Inn, High Street, *c*.1860. It probably dates from the Middle Ages, but its present name only appears in the middle of the 18th century. The Georgian front in the picture looks to have been added to an earlier building with stables on either side. The inn was completely reconstructed *c*.1880 and an hotel (the *Wimbledon Hill*) added later.

143   The *King's Head* Inn, Merton Road, *c*.1900. The inn, on the right of the picture by the cart, claims to date from 1496. It was the scene of a Churchwardens' dinner in 1801 when the bill the parish had to pay was so large that a limit was placed on future dinners. As it was on the Wimbledon boundary (here the Wandle), it was popular as a refuelling stop when the bounds were 'beaten'.

144 The *Rose and Crown* Inn, High Street, 1913. Established about 1650, it was known as the *Sign of the Rose*. After the Restoration of the King in 1660, the word Crown was added. The present building with its twin roof seems to date from the 18th century when the inn became popular and the chief meeting place of the Vestry. The garage on the right has since been demolished to make way for a car park.

145 The *Swan* and the *King of Denmark*, the Ridgway, *c*.1905. Both public houses were started *c*.1860, though the *King* was probably the successor to a beer shop, the *Jolly Gardeners*. The imposing entrance to the *Swan* is said to have come from Cottenham Park House; it has since vanished. Beyond the *King* is Denmark Terrace, a line of shops also built *c*.1860.

146 The *Hand in Hand*, Crooked Billet, *c*.1885. It started in the 1850s as a bakery (which also obliged the neighbours by cooking their mid-day meals for two pence). In the 1870s its owner, Mrs. Holland, took out a licence as a beer retailer. The pub still flourishes.

147 The Welcome Café, on the corner of the High Street and Church Road, *c*.1890. One of the Coffee Taverns set up by the Temperance Movement in the 1870s to try to entice working men from the pubs by providing cheap tea, coffee and cocoa, as well as warmth and reading rooms. The Welcome was the first to be opened and survived the longest—until shortly after 1900.

148 The Village Club and Hall, on the corner of the Ridgway and Lingfield Road, 1925. Designed by Samuel Teulon, they were opened in 1859 to provide 'the opportunities of intellectual and moral improvement, and rational and social enjoyment', through a reading room, library and fortnightly lectures in the Hall (on the left). The Club still flourishes and since 1916 has housed the Wimbledon Society's Museum.

149 Cricket on the Common, 1898. Teams from the volunteer fire brigade and the police sit under an oak tree with the stables of Westside House in the background. Between 1854 and 1890 the Wimbledon Cricket Club had played on the Common, but the pitches were poor and they were glad to move to Wimbledon Park. The Village Club then took over the ground and played there until the 1980s.

150 Wimbledon Town Golf Club: a match on the Common, October 1908, between the Mayor, Councillor C. Walsh (right centre with club) and the Club Captain, George Booth. The Mayor had just opened the new Clubhouse next to the Hermitage in West Place. The Club (now the Wimbledon Common Golf Club) had been formed a few months earlier after the Royal Wimbledon golfers had moved to a new course on the Drax estate to the south.

151 The entrance to the Lawn Tennis Championships in Nursery Road, just off Worple Road, July 1913. The picture is of interest for the dress of the ladies, two cars and their waiting chauffeurs, and above all for the lady selling suffragette literature. During the championships suffragettes tried to set fire to the Centre Court, but were discovered in time.

152 Tea on Court One during the 1913 Championships. It is being served by an army of waitresses to ladies in large Edwardian hats and men mostly in boaters. The building with the ribbed roof and the notice: 'Buffet. Members' is still there. The grounds are now the playing fields of Wimbledon High School.

153 The site of the future All-England tennis courts, 1920. The land had been part of Earl Spencer's dairy farm. It was bought by the All-England Club in 1920 as the Worple Road ground had become too small for the large crowds at the Championships. The picture shows St Mary's church and the large houses in Church Road in the background.

154 The new All-England courts just before their first Championship, 1922. The Centre Court looks very bare; its contractor, Stuarts Granothlithic Co. Ltd., advertises the achievement in the foreground. The outer courts look odd as the bushes round them have only just been planted. To the left is Somerset Road; Church Road is on the right.

Merton Road and Theatre, Wimbledon.

155 Wimbledon Theatre, the Broadway, *c*.1922. Opened on Boxing Day 1910, it had one of the largest stages in the country, lights run off its own power supply and in a basement Turkish baths from which heat could be wafted to the auditorium through ducts. After many ups and downs, it still flourishes with its carved wooden 'angel' above the dome recently restored.

156 The entrance to the King's Palace Cinema, the Broadway, *c*.1914. Wimbledon's second cinema, it opened in 1910 with 400 tip-up seats, 'a complete change of programme' on Mondays and Thursdays, and free teas and light refreshments for those who bought six penny or one shilling seats. It later became a shopping arcade and its site has now been cleared for development.

Hospitals and Health

Hospitals first appear in local records during the 18th century. As there were none locally, poor people like William Bingham were sent up to London; in 1748 he was admitted to St Thomas's 'for curing his broken knee-pan'. Most Wimbledonians, however, preferred to be treated at home by apothecaries like John Sanford.

The first local hospital was founded in 1869 under the will of Mr Atkinson Morley. An ex-medical student at St George's Hospital, he had become proprietor of two leading hotels in London. When he died in 1858, he left £100,000 to St George's 'for receiving, maintaining and generally assisting convalescent poor patients'. With the money the Hospital was able to buy part of the estate of the Earl of Cottenham to the south of Copse Hill and build a large convalescent home for 80 patients. During the Second World War it developed into one of the most advanced brain surgery centres in the world.

For Wimbledon's own needs, however, the Cottage Hospital was even more important. Built on the opposite side of Copse Hill, it was opened less than a year after the Atkinson Morley in May 1870. Its founders were public-spirited men like Dr Gilbert Love and Edward Thurston Holland, whose appeal for donations raised about £1,000. Patients, mainly servants or 'labourers', came with letters of recommendation from regular contributors to its funds. At first more were out-patients as there were only seven beds, a single nurse (the matron) and a kitchen table for operations. Nonetheless, the hospital was said to have won 'considerable favour amongst the working-classes'. It was quiet and homely, and looked after its patients. A similar hospital south of the railway was not opened until 1900. The South Wimbledon, Merton and District Cottage Hospital in Merton Road was also small, but it paved the way for the Nelson Hospital, founded as a permanent memorial of the centenary of Trafalgar in 1905 and opened in 1912.

Behind many of these changes lay the pioneering work of Wimbledon's first Medical Officer of Health, Dr. Evelyn Pocklington. His creation in 1876 of a Fever Hospital for infectious diseases, like scarlet fever, diphtheria and typhoid, in Durnsford Road and its successor, the Isolation Hospital in Gap Road, played a major part in keeping epidemics under control. As a result, by 1914 Wimbledon's death rate was about half the national average and better than all but two of the chief towns in England.

157 Ashford House, High Street, *c.*1900. The home of John Sanford from 1784 until his death in 1855. An apothecary, notable for his work among the poor, he insisted on general inoculation against smallpox. For ordinary illnesses he prescribed 'mixtures, powders and draughts', as well as the great stand-by, bleeding. In 1908 the ground floor was converted into shops. On the right is the smithy.

Wimbledon Cottage Hospital,

FOR NON-INFECTIOUS CASES.

SITUATED—
THURSTAN RD., UPPER WIMBLEDON.

Patients are admitted at all hours.

Accident Cases:
WITHOUT LETTERS OF ADMISSION.

Other Cases:
ON FORMS OF RECOMMENDATION,
To be obtained at the Hospital,
From MRS. THURSTAN HOLLAND, Lady Superintendent,
Lansdowne Road,
From J. F. SCHWANN, ESQ., Honorary Secretary,
Somerset Road,
From MISS WHITTUCK, Mission House, Merton Road,
and others.

An Ambulance stands at the Local Board Offices.

Any Registered Medical man may attend his
own patients at the Hospital.

*In part payment of the expenses of the Hospital, the
following sums are payable weekly by Patients—*

Domestic Servants, 12/6.   Artisan Class, 7/6.
Labouring Class, 5/-.

158 The terms on which patients were admitted to the Cottage Hospital, *c.*1900.

159 The entrance to Wimbledon Hospital, Thurstan Road, 1921. The small Cottage Hospital had been pulled down in 1911 and a new Hospital designed by Sir Thomas Jackson was built. At first it could take only 28 patients, but later this was increased to over seventy. In 1928 a special Children's Wing was added. It was declared redundant in the 1980s. Modern houses now cover the site.

160 Field-Marshal Earl Haig inspecting ex-servicemen when opening a new Nurses' Home at the Hospital, May 1922. Behind him is the Hospital's Chairman, Colonel G.A. Malcolm, D.S.O., a friend of the Field-Marshal under whom he had served in France. In the background are the oak trees of Wimbledon Wood that still covered the land to the west of the Hospital.

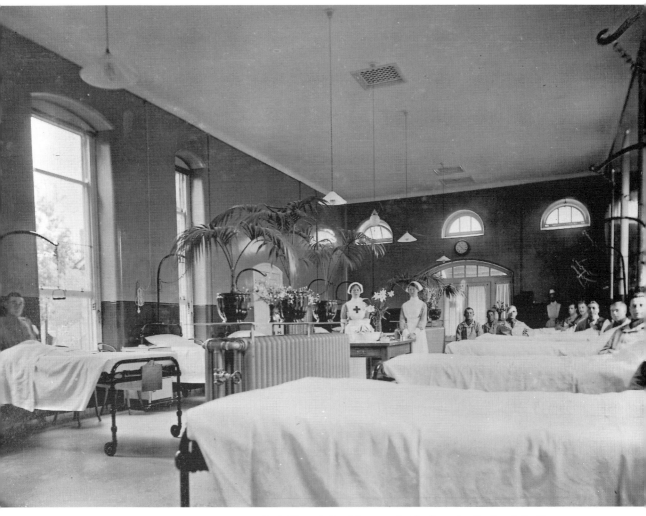

161 A men's ward in Wimbledon Hospital, July 1916. Wounded soldiers, probably from the Battle of the Somme, pose with two nurses in a light, airy ward.

162 'Convalescent Hospital (North Front)', a print dating from *c*.1870, showing the Atkinson Morley shortly after it opened. The view is from Copse Hill. The patients were brought from St George's Hospital, Hyde Park, every Wednesday in two black horse-drawn vehicles with windows along the sides and a door at the back. Those who had completed their week or fortnight's convalescence were then taken back to London.

163 The Nelson Hospital, Kingston Road, at the time of its opening, June 1912. It was set up through the inspiration of a local doctor, Dr. Frank Deas, and designed by F. Hatch. Though not in Wimbledon, it was meant to serve 'Wimbledon, Merton and District' and has cared for many Wimbledonians in the past 80 years. It is now threatened with closure.

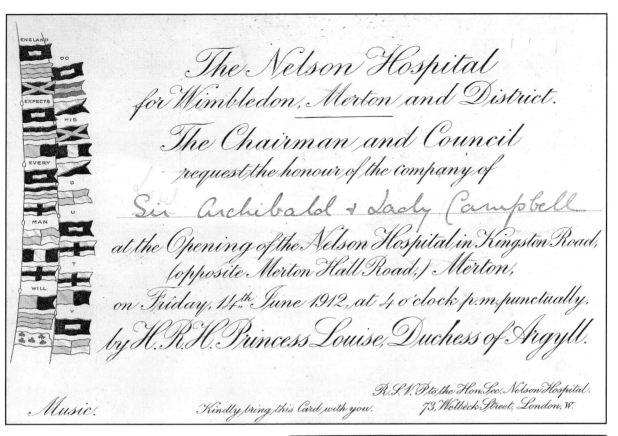

The Nelson Hospital
for Wimbledon, Merton and District.

The Chairman and Council

request the honour of the company of

Sir Archibald & Lady Campbell

at the Opening of the Nelson Hospital in Kingston Road,
(opposite Merton Hall Road,) Merton,
on Friday, 14th June 1912, at 4 o'clock p.m. punctually,
by H.R.H. Princess Louise, Duchess of Argyll.

R.S.V.P to the Hon. Sec. Nelson Hospital.
73, Welbeck Street, London, W.

Music.   Kindly bring this Card with you.

164 Invitation to the opening of the Nelson Hospital,
only 11 months after the foundation stone had been laid
by the Duchess of Sutherland.

165 A Wimbledon nursing sister, Sister Bodfish, about
the time of the First World War.

Two World Wars

Wimbledon was profoundly affected by the wars. For the first time every family was involved in some direct way and by 1945 'the life of leisured ease in beautiful surroundings', which had existed at least in parts of the borough, had gone for good.

'The Kaiser's War' (1914-18) was notable for the first air raids, by Zeppelins and then by Gotha heavy bombers. But they only dropped one bomb on Wimbledon. It fell in a field along the Ridgway and failed to explode. The war also led to the commandeering of a large area on the Common for use as an Army training camp and as a temporary fighter base. Equally important was the finding of homes for over eight hundred Belgian refugees, some of whom remained here after the war was over. But perhaps the two most unpleasant effects of the war were the food shortages and the deaths of so many young men. In 1917 Britain was nearly starved into surrender by German U-boat attacks and the Government was forced belatedly to introduce rationing. The terrible casualties among servicemen, above all in the fighting on the Western Front, affected a large number of families in Wimbledon. Those who died were commemorated by a War Memorial on the edge of the Common, unveiled in 1921, and by a new Warrior Chapel in St Mary's.

'Hitler's War' (1939-45) was even more dramatic in its effects. The Blitz of 1940-41, followed by the V-1 flying bombs in the summer of 1944, totally demolished over six hundred houses and badly damaged about half the remainder. The number of casualties was surprisingly low, thanks to the many air-raid shelters and the efficiency of the rescue services. But many families left Wimbledon. The children who stayed had their lessons regularly interrupted by air-raid warnings. Their mothers had to go off to the shops for food, most of it 'on the ration' and no longer delivered to the door. Their fathers, if not called up for the Army, had to serve in the Home Guard or A.R.P., as well as fire-watching at home. They could find 'a good lunch' at one of the British Restaurants, or grow their own vegetables in one of the allotments that were developed in parks, recreation grounds and even on the Common. But a visit to the pub was little help as war-time beer was said to be 'appalling' and escape to the country in the family car was impossible as petrol was not available for 'pleasure motoring'.

VE Day in May 1945, therefore, saw wilder rejoicings than on any previous occasion in Wimbledon's long history.

166   Searchlights over Wimbledon station, probably in 1915. The picture has been taken from Hill Road towards the station forecourt, with the booking office in the centre and the bridge on the right. The searchlights are looking for Zeppelins, whose most unpleasant raid was on 13 October 1915. None of their bombs fell on Wimbledon, but explosions elsewhere could clearly be seen from the top of the hill.

167 Part of the Army Camp on the Common, near Caesar's Well, 1918. In the foreground is 'the garden', used for growing cabbages. In the background are four Army lorries standing by an administration hut with civilian cars nearby. The Camp was used from the winter of 1916 for the training of troops before they were sent overseas. So parts of the Common were criss-crossed with trenches, as well as a 'bayonetting ground'.

168 The Allotments on the Common opposite West Place, July 1918. Many allotments were set up during the War, particularly when potatoes and vegetables became scarce in 1917. This one extended across to Parkside, north of the Causeway (on the right). On the left clothes from local laundries dry in the wind. In the background is the large Y.M.C.A. hut used to entertain the troops.

169 Tank Day outside the Town Hall, 14 March 1918. A large crowd are being encouraged to invest in War Bonds by the presence of one of the Army's latest tanks, which had distinguished themselves the previous November at the Battle of Cambrai. Only a week after this photograph was taken the Germans broke through the British front north of the Somme and nearly won the war.

170 The Piggery in Wimbledon Park, August 1918, with King George V and Queen Mary presented with a piglet. The Queen looks delighted. The Mayor, Alderman Allen, stands next to her wearing his chain of office. As in the Second World War, pig-keeping was encouraged to increase the supply of food.

171 The Ceremonial Unveiling of the War Memorial, Parkside, 1 November 1921. Designed by Sir Thomas Jackson, it was unveiled by the M.P. for Wimbledon, Sir Joseph Hood (who stands to the left of the Mayor, Alderman Stuart, at the base of the Memorial). To the right Canon Monroe conducts a religious service, with the choir from St Mary's in the foreground.

172 Air-raid practice in the summer of 1939. An Ursuline Convent girl leads the way into a shelter wearing a gas mask. A fear of gas attack was then as great as the expectation of massive air raids and all civilians were issued with gas masks. They were never needed, which is doubly fortunate as their filters were made from asbestos fibre.

173 The Gun-site on the Common, 1945. Two 4.5-inch anti-aircraft guns were stationed near the Windmill in 1940. Together with the battery of guns in Prince George's Playing Fields, Raynes Park, they fired a deafening barrage at German planes during the night blitz, showering jagged steel splinters and large nose-cones all over Wimbledon and damaging roofs.

174 A queue outside a butcher's in Arthur Road, 1941. The shop window is partly boarded up; the display seems to be of fresh eggs. The customers had to be registered for meat and eggs at this shop; they could not buy them elsewhere. Favoured customers might also get sausages. So it was worth cultivating the butchers, especially as meat was 'on the ration' until 1954.

175 A British Restaurant, South Wimbledon, 1944. In the background is a mural by John Piper, since destroyed. A first 'Communal Feeding Centre' in Wimbledon was set up in Holy Trinity Church Hall, the Broadway, in the autumn of 1940. Others followed in Haydons Road, Raynes Park, Merton Road, the High Street and Arthur Road. They provided meals off-ration at about one shilling.

176 The final parade of the Home Guard, November 1944. Like their predecessors in the Napoleonic Wars, the Home Guard trained on the Common (criss-crossed with trenches and posts to prevent gliders landing). They manned concrete pill-boxes and carried out night patrols. In the autumn of 1944 they were 'stood down' after this last parade, with the salute taken by their commanding officer, Lieut.-Col. W. Tenison, D.S.O. in front of Elys.

177 The Prisoner-of-War Camp, Southside, 1946. Italians and later Germans were kept in this small camp on the Common, opposite the end of Lauriston Road. They were employed on the land or in local factories, and in their spare time built this wooden model of the Windmill. In the background of the photograph is Chester House.

178 A Victory Street Party, Stroud Road, Wimbledon Park, May 1945. All over Wimbledon the end of the War was greeted with understandable joy. Giant bonfires were lit on the Common, there was dancing in the streets and children's parties were held in many places, as here. The Civil Defence and Armed Services later held a Victory Parade to the Town Hall.

Wimbledon since 1945

Recovery from the war was slow. There was continued food and clothes rationing, as well as acute shortages of houses and fuel. Bombed-sites were filled with 'pre-fabs', while many shop windows were still boarded up after the air raids.

Yet life was not all gloom. A Community Association organised a Drama Festival in the Civic Hall, a Community Centre was built in St George's Road and a Symphony Orchestra was founded. In 1948 the Council took over Cannizaro House as an Old People's Home and opened its fine grounds as a public park.

New houses or blocks of flats began to be built, including a large estate behind Chester and Westside Houses on the Common. Many old houses were converted into flats or, like those along Parkside, pulled down and their grounds filled with smaller 'town houses'.

South Wimbledon too became more attractive as a residential area. The disappearance of the Gas, Sewage and Electricity Works helped, while the advent of the Smokeless Zone meant that 'smogs' were a thing of the past.

By the early 1960s post-war austerity had given way to growing affluence. The shops were once more well stocked and supermarkets flourished. The cinemas suffered, however, from the growing competition of television, while the Theatre was saved from redevelopment only by the intervention of the Council.

Even the creation of the London Borough of Merton in 1965 did not stop Wimbledon's own development. A Children's Theatre opened on the Broadway; the Windmill on the Common was turned into a museum; and a Lawn Tennis Museum was started at the All-England Club. Above all, by the middle 1970s over forty per cent of households in Wimbledon were said to have a car and regular traffic jams blocked the Broadway, Hill Road and the High Street.

Over the centuries Wimbledon has changed, at times dramatically. For some people 'it has lost much of its dignity and serenity'. Yet the character of the area has survived even the rush of modern traffic. It is still, as one resident has remarked, 'a very pleasant place in which to live'.

179 West Place, Wimbledon, 1985. These old cottages are a good example of the way 'desirable areas' of Wimbledon have gone 'up market' since the Second World War. Built in the 1840s for about £100 each, they are now considered ideal retirement homes and are offered by estate agents at over £300,000. In 1992 their front gardens won the London in Bloom award and were visited by the Queen Mother.

180 A fire at Woolworth's, the Broadway, April 1981. Despite all the efforts of the firemen, the shop was completely burnt out (but has since been rebuilt). Over the centuries fires have destroyed important buildings in Wimbledon: the Marlborough manor house in 1785, Cannizaro in 1900, the High School in 1917, St Mark's church in 1966 and Wimbledon College hall in 1977.

181 The shops on the Bridge, *c.*1970. They illustrate the short life-expectancy of buildings in modern Wimbledon. Put up in the early 1930s, those on the left of the bridge, together with most of those on Hill Road up to Elys, have since been pulled down and replaced by modern glass-fronted blocks. Traffic too has transformed the area, with a stream of buses, cars and lorries pouring over the bridge today.

182 A crowd, mostly young, waiting to greet the Queen at the top of Wimbledon Hill, July 1977. In her Silver Jubilee year she was on her way to watch the Ladies Singles final at the Centenary Championships, won by Virginia Wade. Nearly 400 years earlier a much smaller crowd probably stood here to watch Elizabeth I drive past on her way to Nonsuch Palace after visiting Sir Thomas Cecil at his new manor house.

Main Sources

Curry, C., *Memories of my side of the Common* (1988)

Milward, R.J., *A New Short History of Wimbledon* (1989)

Milward, R.J., *Historic Wimbledon: From Caesar's Camp to Centre Court* (1989)

Plastow, N., *Safe as Houses, Wimbledon,1939-45* (1972)

Plastow, N., (ed.), *A History of Wimbledon and Putney Commons* (1988)

Wimbledon Society Museum, Minutes of Local History Group, 1971-94; Local Directories and Maps

Map of Wimbledon in 1890. Published by Stanford.